Better Homes and Gardens®

GARAGES BASEMENTS & ATTICS

© Copyright 1985 by Meredith Corporation, Des Moines, Iowa.
All Rights Reserved. Printed in the United States of America.
First Edition. First Printing.
Library of Congress Catalog Card Number: 85-60586
ISBN: 0-696-02179-X

BETTER HOMES AND GARDENS® BOOKS

Editor: Gerald M. Knox
Art Director: Ernest Shelton
Managing Editor: David A. Kirchner
Copy and Production Editors: Marsha Jahns, Mary Helen Schiltz,
Carl Voss, David A. Walsh

Associate Art Directors: Linda Ford Vermie, Neoma Alt West,
Randall Yontz
Assistant Art Directors: Lynda Haupert, Harijs Priekulis,
Tom Wegner
Senior Graphic Designers: Mike Eagleton, Lyne Neymeyer,
Stan Sams
Graphic Designers: Mike Burns, Sally Cooper, Darla Whipple-Frain,
Brian Wignall

Vice President, Editorial Director: Doris Eby
Group Editorial Services Director: Duane L. Gregg

Senior Vice President, General Manager: Fred Stines
Director of Publishing: Robert B. Nelson
Vice President, Retail Marketing: Jamie Martin
Vice President, Direct Marketing: Arthur Heydendael

All About Your House: Garages, Basements, and Attics

Project Editor: James A. Hufnagel
Associate Editors: Willa Rosenblatt Speiser, Leonore A. Levy
Copy and Production Editor: David Walsh
Building and Remodeling Editor: Joan McCloskey
Furnishings and Design Editor: Shirley Van Zante
Garden Editor: Douglas A. Jimerson
Money Management and Features Editor: Margaret Daly

Associate Art Director: Randall Yontz
Graphic Designer: Alisann Dixon
Electronic Text Processor: Donna Russell

Contributing Editors: Stephen Mead and Jill Abeloe Mead
Contributors: John Ingersoll, Marsha Jahns, Dan Kaercher,
Paul Kitzke, Nancy Nowiszewski, Michael Scott, Carl Voss,
Michael Walsh

Special thanks to William N. Hopkins, Bill Hopkins, Jr.,
Babs Klein, Linda Ford Vermie, and Don Wipperman for their
valuable contributions to this book.

INTRODUCTION

In too many homes, garages, basements, and attics are orphans. Dim, drab, and consigned to storing things that should have been thrown out years ago—that's the usual fate of these spaces. Their potential for serving your family normally goes untapped. If you've intended to "do something" about your house's unfinished areas, but are unsure just how to get started, this book is for you.

Garages, basements, and attics by nature aren't glamorous places. They house cars and garden gear, furnaces, water heaters, and laundry equipment, outgrown clothes and toys, suitcases, and Christmas decorations. If this is all you want your home's peripheral spaces to do, how can you organize and equip them for greater efficiency? *Garages, Basements, & Attics* examines the utility aspects of each, tells how to solve problems in these areas, and suggests ways you can increase productivity up, down, or out there.

Need more living space? Finishing unfinished space almost always costs less than adding on—not only up front, but also later when you add in higher energy expenses and possible property tax increases. More than 100 drawings and color photographs show the possibilities for developing "found spaces," and dozens more take you step by step through the process of converting them.

Or perhaps your biggest problem is that you simply don't have enough space for the stuff you need to store. Adding an attic or basement usually doesn't make economic sense, but planning and building a new garage is easier than you might think. An entire chapter shows and tells what is involved.

Garages, Basements, & Attics is one in a series of books in the **ALL ABOUT YOUR HOUSE** Library, a comprehensive encyclopedia of home planning, decorating, building, and management. Additional volumes in the series delve with equal thoroughness into other aspects of your home.

GARAGES,
BASEMENTS,
& ATTICS

CONTENTS

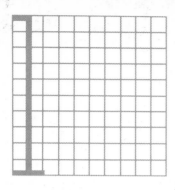

SURVEY YOUR HOME'S UNFINISHED ZONES

Your home may house three big space wasters: its garage, basement, and attic. If any one of these areas isn't working as hard for you as it should, read on. This chapter takes you on a tour of all three, helps you analyze the potential of each, and guides you to pages later in the book that can help you turn possibilities into practical, livable realities. Let's get started. All you need bring along is a pad and pencil to note your ideas, and perhaps a flashlight to help you see a few diamonds in the rough—areas that you can turn into sparkling living spaces with some imagination and work.

COULD YOU MAKE YOUR BASEMENT BRIGHT AND CHEERY?

Basements are the first unfinished areas most homeowners turn to when they need more living space.

That's what the owners of the attractive room shown here did, deciding in the process to play up a basement feature most finishers choose to hide. Rather than cover up the joists overhead, they added blocking between them, painted everything up there black, then trimmed the underside with 1x2s. The result is the reverse of a suspended ceiling, and saves valuable headroom.

Sizing up your basement

Before you even can begin to think about converting a basement to living space, it has to satisfy several important requirements:

• Is there enough headroom down there? The minimum needed for comfort and building codes is 7½ feet; a few pipes or heating ducts could drop below this height, but you may want to plan to place tables, seating, or other low-profile features beneath them.
• Does your basement have moisture problems? Leaks, seepage, and sweating walls can wreck improvements you make belowground. To learn about drying out a wet basement, see pages 148 and 149.
• How's light, ventilation, and access down there? Pages 146 and 147 discuss these important topics.

For specifics about planning a basement conversion, see pages 76-79 in Chapter 5— "Getting the Space Ready." More examples of basement conversions appear on pages 38-41, 68-71, and 88-91.

DOES YOUR FAMILY NEED A PLACE TO GET TOGETHER?

You almost certainly have a living room, and very likely a dining room, too. If you have children, they probably have a playroom, or at least a room so full of toys that by any other name it is still a playroom. But when all is said and done, is there a room in your home where all members of the family can gather on a rainy afternoon? A place that has enough space for everyone, and enough amenities to keep them all happy? If not, consider the possibility of turning one of the unfinished spaces at your house into just such a haven.

When you're thinking about creating a room for the family, give your imagination free rein. Durable materials and reasonably cleanable surfaces make sense in any room meant for leisure-time use, but this doesn't rule out sleek design, thoughtful details, and an overall look of casual elegance. The below-grade family center pictured *at right* proves the point.

Here, a full-scale lower-level remodeling created an open-plan area with a spacious, airy layout that more than makes up for its subterranean location. Your own plans for a family center may be more limited, or it may be your garage or attic you're thinking of converting. Nevertheless, this project has several features worth adapting.

Consider, for example, the attractive wooden stairs. If you're going to convert all or part of a basement into living space, try to make a visual plus out of the inevitable stairway. Similarly, if you have a slanted ceiling in your attic, build your decorating case around its charm, rather than focusing on the limited headroom along the kneewalls.

Providing at least a secondary food preparation area is something to think about, too. You might want nothing more than a pint-size refrigerator and a sink, but even a minimal "kitchen" will make both family gatherings and informal entertaining more relaxing.

For other examples of family centers created out of unfinished, underused house or garage space, see pages 30-33, 38-39, and 64-67. To learn more about making a new family center even more inviting, see Chapter 8—"Special Features."

WHAT ARE YOUR OPTIONS FOR A NEW BEDROOM?

Given a comfortable bed, you can get a good night's sleep almost anywhere. For most of us, however, attractive surroundings and amenities such as storage, seating, and an attached bath are something more than absolute necessities, yet less than pure luxuries. If your family is outgrowing its home or you lack space for guests, you may wonder where you'll ever find space for even another basic bedroom, let alone a new bath. Don't despair, however. Your house's unfinished zones may have just the space you need. Here are a few places and ways to start searching for it.

The appealing master suite pictured *opposite* and *above* is almost a textbook example of how to turn an attic into an attractive new bedroom. When the homeowners decided they needed another bedroom and thought of turning their attic into a self-contained suite, they took on several remodeling tasks.

Although a dormer had been added years before, most of the upstairs space was cramped and poorly lit. The owners raised the dormer's roof so it matched the roofline of the rest of the house, then replaced a series of small, separate, south-facing windows with the row of large sliding units shown *above.* Adding a few extra feet of headroom and a lot of sunshine changed not only the

way the attic looks but also the way it lives.

To take advantage of all available floor space, the owners installed custom-made built-ins that tuck neatly under the room's sloping ceiling. As shown *opposite,* the recessed bookcase runs between the bed and the storage divider.

Finding potential bedrooms in unfinished areas

If you don't have an attic or the attic you have is already being put to good use, you may wonder whether your garage or basement has potential as sleeping space. They probably do. Keep in mind that in a basement you may have to improve light and ventilation and that in a garage you may have to extend one or more utilities to make the space livable and comfortable.

In all cases, be especially careful to abide by local housing and building codes. Many municipalities require a certain amount of window space in proportion to floor space, and a certain minimum floor space as well. Remember, also, that fire safety is a key factor in determining whether space is suitable for sleeping; you may have to add a secondary escape route if you plan to convert an attic or basement to sleeping space. (A garage is more likely already to have more than one means of exit.) See pages 29 and 95 for more about legal and safety matters.

For some interesting examples of newly finished sleeping quarters, see pages 24-27. Pages 28-29 and 40-41 go a step further and feature unfinished spaces that became full-fledged apartments.

CAN YOUR GARAGE DO MORE THAN HOUSE CARS?

There's no denying the benefits of a garage for housing your cars, especially if you live in a harsh climate, have a particularly prized car, or just dislike having autos on permanent display in the street or driveway. However, if you can readily find another good place to keep your family's vehicles, then you may be tempted to turn your garage to other uses. And if space for people or possessions other than cars is tight at your house, trading in your one-job garage for a multipurpose space could be a temptation worth yielding to.

The family room featured here offers a combination of period charm and entertainment-oriented convenience. At first or even second glance, neither the exterior nor the interior bears much resemblance to a garage—but look again.

Survey the small photograph *above* and you'll see that the iron-muntined sliding glass doors match the size of the opening on a single-door two-car garage. Where the driveway of this drive-under garage once split the backyard in two, now are a poured concrete patio and a newly made lawn.

Inside, the transformation is just as complete. Ash wainscoting, hollow-core beams, a fireplace of salvage-yard brick, and textured walls provide a comfortable setting for family gatherings as well as for larger social occasions. Tucked into one corner of the room is a bar, complete with slate counter and ash woodwork. It provides storage and includes a sink, ice maker, and compact refrigerator.

This is only one approach to turning your garage into living space. For other examples, see pages 30-33 and 96-99. To find out about the planning and actual work involved in a project of this nature, see pages 64-67 and 84-87.

What will work for you?
Whether your garage is detached, side-by-side, or drive-under determines at least in part the best way you might expand its function. A garage that's detached but within a few yards of the house would work well as a bedroom, for example. Or, you could turn it into an attached garage, connected to your home by newly enclosed living space. A garage way back in the yard, however, may be suitable only for use as a guest cottage or workroom.

Storage is something any type of garage can provide, however, and often without putting your car out on the street. For more about maximizing the storage potential of your garage, see pages 52 and 53. And for some ideas about a partial garage conversion that goes beyond storage but stops short of eliminating cars, see pages 36 and 37.

IS YOUR GARAGE A CANDIDATE FOR CONVERSION?

When you consider your garage's conversion potential, several questions come to mind. First, is your garage physically suitable? Is it large enough to convert? Is it attached to your home, or at least close enough to attach without great expense? Are some or all utilities already connected? If not, is it feasible to extend them? What will you do with your cars if you turn your garage into something else? Can you do without a garage completely? Could a carport provide sufficient shelter for your vehicles? If not, does it make financial sense to build a new garage? If the answers to these questions suggest that your garage does indeed have a great future as a living area, you have some exciting planning, as well as some hard work, ahead.

The comfortable garden room pictured *opposite* and the deck adjacent to it, shown *above*, do wonders for the livability of the 50-year-old house they're part of. When you consider that the rear portion of this home once was a garage and a cramped, small-windowed mudroom, the improvement seems even more dramatic.

An appealing combination of dark-finished woodwork and smooth-textured, off-white walls creates a pleasantly informal, warm look in the new room. And thanks to careful attention to detail—using salvaged trim from the old garage to frame the new opening, for example—the exterior effect is equally pleasing.

Note the skylight-pierced cathedral ceiling that gives the room so much of its charm. Cathedral ceilings are common features in garage conversions since they are a good way to turn a negative architectural feature into a positive one. That's because many garages have 7-foot-high wall studs; a flat, 7-foot ceiling would be too low for comfort, and certainly wouldn't give the sense of space you'd expect to have after transforming a garage into house space.

Consider your own options

If you've come to the conclusion that your garage is both convertible and dispensable, you're ready to do some preliminary planning. Not until you have a general idea of what you want should you call in a professional to help you with the specifics of design or construction. A professional, after all, can only tell you what's feasible from an architectural, engineering, or financial standpoint once given some idea of what you're trying to achieve.

Be clear about the kind of living space you want, what amenities you'd like to install, any second-stage plans you might have for the space, how much you can spend at this time, and so on. To find out more about this vital early planning stage, see Chapter 4—"Planning Bonus Spaces."

You can probably do all or most of a garage conversion project on your own. The walls that support the structure are already in place, so the remaining work is largely a matter of dividing and finishing space. The only outside consultation absolutely necessary is to check local building and housing codes. You need to make sure the room's new function and your conversion methods are permitted. For advice about setting up and carrying through a do-it-yourself conversion, see Chapter 5—"Getting the Space Ready"—and Chapter 9—"Extending Services."

WOULD A NEW GARAGE SOLVE YOUR SPACE CRUNCH?

Perhaps your house was built without a garage. Or, perhaps your house once had a garage, but it became living space because people room was more important than car storage. Maybe you have a compact one-car garage and a couple of larger-than-compact cars. Whatever the reason, you may feel that a new garage would make a welcome addition to your property. Happily, building one is cheaper and easier than you probably think.

Once you've decided that your cars need shelter, the next step is to find out whether your lot has enough room for a new structure. Then you need to make sure any building you plan to do meets all municipal standards and zoning regulations.

Finally, you must decide who'll do the work. Would you like to tackle the project alone, get an architect to plan the structure for you, or put the entire job in the hands of professionals? How you answer this question depends on several factors, including your own how-to expertise, how much money you can devote to the project, and how important the appearance of the garage is to you. If you plan to do any part of the job yourself or just want to understand what your builder is doing and why, you'll find lots of useful information in Chapter 7—"Garages Just for Cars."

How will it look?
You may be comfortable with the practical aspect of building a new garage. After all, it offers not only the prospect of a warm, dry shelter for your car, but also the chance to create better storage, a workroom at one end of the structure, or some other extra. You may wonder, however, how to fit a new building or good-size addition to your home into the overall layout and style of your home and property.

The added-on garage featured *at left* reflects one popular approach. Here, the original garage had become a playroom. Several years later, the homeowners decided they'd like to keep their cars indoors again, so they built a new garage in front of the original one. This decision saved them some work, too. They still could use the old driveway.

HOW EASILY
CAN YOU REACH
YOUR ATTIC?

Most homes have at least a crawl space above the top living level. And where there's space, there's almost certainly a way to get up there. Unfortunately, the way may be nothing more than a fold-up staircase that drops from a hallway ceiling, or a plain trap door that requires setting up a ladder whenever you want to reach the attic. If you plan to do something more with your attic than insulate it and close it off, you may need to improve or even relocate its entrance.

The cozy loft pictured *at left* started out as part of an unfinished attic in a small, 1½-story home. In the course of a whole-house remodeling, the owners gave up a downstairs bedroom for the sake of a larger dining area. That spurred their decision to develop the unused upper level of their home, creating both a master suite and the den/guest room featured here.

Although not originally designed as living space, the attic did have a 9-foot-high ridge line and a pair of gable-end windows. This gave it ample headroom and some light and ventilation. What the attic lacked, however, was finished surfaces and ready access from the floor below.

Drywall, natural wood, and a handsome open stairway were the answers to the attic's—and the homeowners'—needs. The gallery rail visible in the right part of the photograph is a continuation of the stair rail. The stairs themselves are just out of camera range, at a right angle to the loft's main part.

If you're planning to make greater use of an upstairs crawl space or full-height but unfinished attic, you'll want to consider upstairs and downstairs traffic patterns when deciding what kind of access you need and how it affects household traffic. If, for example, you're hoping to create a super-efficient storage space upstairs, you may not need a full-time, full-service stairway. A sturdy set of hidden stairs may do just fine. But for a multilevel living space that receives daily traffic, you'll want at least a spiral staircase.

For more about improving access to attics, see pages 72-75 and 152-153; for more about finishing upstairs spaces and installing new surfaces, see pages 80-83.

CAN YOU OVERCOME AN ATTIC'S LIMITATIONS?

One of the charms of attic space is its unexpected angles, its nooks and crannies, and escapes from the ordinary. Put less positively, this means attics often come in odd shapes and are too narrow or irregular for standard furnishings in conventional arrangements. Add to this ceilings too close to the floor to allow for normal traffic patterns, and you see that attics can present real design challenges. There's almost always a way around these obstacles, however—the trick is to find the solution that best fits your attic and your needs.

If you're hoping to work within existing attic space, the guest room shown *at left* is a good example of what you can do. Here, seating, sleeping, and storage occupy the low-headroom zones along the walls; paths between the furniture take advantage of full-height areas toward the center of the room.

A more radical although hardly revolutionary approach to "expanding" your attic is to make a structural change. That usually means building a dormer or two. Depending on the size and style you choose, a dormer can do anything from providing you with a cozy window seat to doubling upstairs living space.

Adding a dormer or working within existing space usually calls for at least 10 feet of headroom at the highest point in the attic.

If the height is less than that, creating living space in your attic may be difficult: The result will always be somewhat cramped, unless you want to literally raise the roof, which will give added height on all sides. This isn't as farfetched as it sounds, though it certainly calls for skilled workers.

To see a variety of attic transformations, turn to pages 22-29. If improved storage rather than extra living space is your goal, see pages 48 and 49. For additional inspiration, look at pages 92-95, where you'll find a case study of an especially successful dormer. And if you're thinking of building a dormer yourself, turn to pages 116 and 117 for good advice and instruction.

A POTPOURRI OF USES

Now that you've appraised the unfinished spaces at your house, it's time to evaluate their potential to fill your family's unmet living needs. An unfinished attic, basement, or garage— or even open space between your house and garage—is unmined gold to ingenious remodelers who know what they want. The challenge is to view these taken-for-granted utility areas through unclouded eyes. Look past the cars, the boxes, and the clutter to potential living spaces that are ripe for remodeling. That's what this chapter is all about. We'll show you how others applied imagination and elbow grease to get the bonus spaces they always wanted—without costly additions. In many instances, the homeowners' monetary investment was minimal; their vision, however, was big and bold.

AN ATTIC REFURBISHED FOR MUSIC PRACTICE

A music room may sound like a luxurious extra that belongs only in a rambling—if not palatial— home, but that's not necessarily the case. The compact conservatory pictured here, for example, tops off a standard 1950s ranch house.

Spectacularly understated is an apt description for this 12x20-foot attic-turned-music-loft. Sunlight streaming through newly installed windows and skylights defines the room's spare lines. Further enhancing the visual elegance is the interplay of white walls and natural-wood floor and ceiling.

Rather than isolate their attic gem, these homeowners decided to trade off some loft space for an open ceiling above the living room. This maneuver called for a railing that wouldn't limit the newly created interior vista any more than necessary. An innovative railing with a nautical theme was the solution. It's made of stainless steel wire and tubular posts, purchased from a boat supplier. A final design bonus: A stately fan-shaped window that adds both sunlight and distinction.

If you're thinking about turning unused space into a music room but don't want to raise the noise level in other rooms, soundproof your music space. First make sure that the new floor will be acoustically independent from the ceiling below. Fill the joist cavities with fiberglass insulation, and add a carpet with a heavy pad for further soundproofing. If you plan to subdivide your attic or loft space, beef up walls with fiberglass batts and a layer of soundboard, or further break the transmission of sound by staggering studs so they don't touch each other.

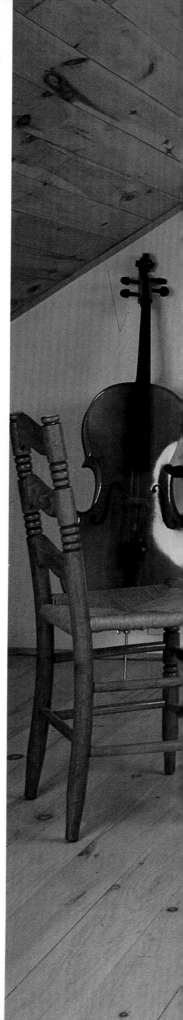

AN ATTIC MASTER BEDROOM

The need to steal some solitude in an active household is probably as old as the concept of family itself. Often, an attic lends itself particularly well to use as a retreat, whether for adults, teenagers, or children just old enough to want a special place of their own. The attic's center usually has enough headroom to accommodate even the tallest householder, and smart remodelers make the most of awkward attic nooks and corners to carve out efficient storage niches and window openings.

What parents wouldn't want a private suite like this aerie nestled in the former attic of a compact Tudor-style home? It has space to lounge, to think, and to recharge—all away from the bustle of a busy household.

With the help of many sheets of drywall and four new dormers, the owners carved their master bedroom out of steeply angled spaces. The core of this new suite is the handsome, clean-lined sleep/sitting area pictured *opposite*. During the day, it's awash with natural light from two new dormers; at night, track lighting provides illumination. There's

no wasted under-eave space here—it's all claimed by low shelving and storage units that keep possessions on the perimeter.

This retreat also includes a skylit compartmented bath, shown *above*. Tucked into under-eave and dormer space, it's divided into three areas— toilet and shower, walk-in closet, and dressing room. A low tiled platform along the outside walls of the bath surrounds a large built-in tub. The home's original brick walls are exposed in the bath and elsewhere in the attic to contrast with the drywall-finished white ceilings and the carpeted floors.

Geometry makes an important contribution to the room's beauty—the familiar sharp

corners and angles of an attic make this space all the more interesting and inviting. Finishing off such tall, sloping walls can be one of the biggest design challenges in an attic remodeling, however.

Dormer types

There are two basic types of dormers—shed and gable. *Gable dormers,* used in this remodeling, have peaked roofs projecting at right angles to the main roof. A *shed dormer* has a single sloping roof that projects out from the main roof at a shallower angle. Shed dormers can be much wider than gables, and they're cheaper to build.

Constructing new attic dormers involves removing some of the original roof, framing in the dormer spaces, and reroofing. To find the best place to install dormers, go up on the roof and simply imagine looking out (or neighbors looking in) from different angles. For more about dormers, see pages 116 and 117.

Other possibilities

Dormers aren't the only way to let light into an attic and increase your living space. The minimal approach involves adding only windows and skylights without altering the existing roof structure.

Raising the roof is a more drastic attack: Part of the roof is replaced by a shed dormer at a shallower pitch but with a higher ridge. The most extensive and expensive alternative is to raise the roof and add a completely new second or third level. This offers attic remodelers an opportunity to add 50 to 100 percent to a home's square footage.

AN ATTIC
REMODELED
FOR TEENAGERS

If you have older children or teenagers at your house, you know just how important an asset privacy can be. The two preceding pages show an attic transformed into an adult master suite. Here's another way to go—a room at the top especially for teens.

Beneath the peaked ceiling and the down-to-the-floor eaves of this attic hideaway is room for a teen to study, read, fiddle with the sound system, or just daydream—all thanks to a creative attic remodeling.

Each of the four gables in this attic is assigned a specific function—sleeping, studying, dressing, or bathing—creating what amounts to a separate suite. As with many other attic remodelings, white-painted drywall was the space-stretching choice for walls and ceilings, except in the sleeping alcove, which is made cozier by batik fabric applied to the walls and ceiling. Exposed gable supports add architectural interest to the far end of the study nook.

A sturdy iron railing, painted bright red for accent, overlooks the dining room and entry below. The entire first floor of this house was also transformed by splashes of light from the new attic roof window and the opened-up ceiling.

Access to the new upstairs level is via a compact circular staircase tucked into a corner of the dining room. Just 48 inches in diameter, the staircase makes an interesting visual accent without stealing a large amount of floor space from main living areas.

Here, as is often found in attics in small homes, limited headroom dictated that furniture line the room's perimeter. How much space do you need to avoid bumping into a wall at every turn? The answer depends on your specific plans and on local code requirements. Generally speaking, you should have at least 8 feet directly below the roof's ridge line and about 4 feet of height at knee walls.

AN ATTIC
TURNED INTO
AN APARTMENT

If you're fortunate enough to possess an abundance of attic space, why limit yourself to creating a single room? You may be able, local zoning permitting, to tuck a complete apartment under your roof. Whether you hope to create an income-producing unit or would just like to carve out comfortable living quarters for a semi-independent family member, you'll find it takes extra planning to subdivide spaces for maximum efficiency. But the rewards, both financial and aesthetic, are worth the effort.

The attic apartment featured on these two pages combines under-the-eaves charm with everyday convenience. Originally a large third-floor attic, it consisted of a hallway and a central 10x16-foot room with a flat ceiling. Because the house has a steeply pitched hip roof, much of the unfinished attic along the perimeter of the upstairs area also had generous headroom.

The first step in this attic conversion was to tear down the walls that separated the central room from the peripheral spaces. Installing a vapor barrier and insulating the attic walls and ceiling were next on the list of priorities, followed by the most dramatic phase of the transformation: Walls were sheathed in rough-sawn pine for warmth and textural interest. It took extra work, but the wall treatment definitely sparks the warmth the owners wanted.

Even though this is a large attic, only careful use of space made enough room for a full-facility apartment. Perimeter built-ins were used wherever feasible. The photo *opposite* shows built-in seating units lining the under-eave area; the dining nook, complete with a built-in booth, is brightened by an operable new skylight.

For areas where maximum headroom was necessary, the remodelers turned to two large existing dormers. The kitchen, pictured *above,* is visually enlarged by shiny white finishes. An all-in-one kitchen unit encompasses counter space, sink, range, and storage for dinnerware and utensils.

MAKING IT LEGAL

Here are the three major aspects to consider before you convert a garage, basement, or attic into a rental unit.

• *Zoning ordinances* are a key factor. If you wish to use a portion of your home in a way not permitted under your town's zoning, such as a rental unit in a one-family zone, you will need a variance. Read zoning rules carefully, then discuss them with someone who knows about such matters—either an attorney or a member of the town's zoning board.

• *Building codes* govern materials and methods of construction and apply no matter what the zoning is. Even if you live in an area that permits rental units, make sure yours will meet all code requirements. Again, check codes, then talk with an expert.

• *Housing codes* are general rules designed to protect public health, safety, welfare, and often, property values. Housing codes dictate matters such as mimimum sizes for sleeping rooms, amount of window space, and so forth. Just as your home must meet these standards, so must all other dwelling units.

Keep in mind that many zoning ordinances specify how much off-street parking is allowed on a given lot, and where it may be placed.

A DRIVE-UNDER
GARAGE CONVERTED
TO FAMILY SPACE

As much as your car deserves a warm, dry place to stay in bad weather, there comes a time when family convenience may have to take precedence. If you have a garage in your basement—the kind sometimes known as a drive-under garage— you may have an ideal candidate for conversion to living space. If you need a family room, hobby center, or other leisure-time quarters, you may want to borrow some ideas from the family room transformation featured here.

Thanks to its back-sloping lot, the compact Colonial home pictured on these two pages had lots of prime lower-level space ideally suited to family living. For years, however, that space belonged to the family car, while the family itself did without an informal family activity area— and also did without direct access to their backyard from the ground level.

With the help of an architect, the homeowners designed a conversion that fits right into the home's original look, keeping the conversion from looking like a conversion. Sliding glass doors now fill the space the garage door once occupied. Skillful planning and landscaping help to make the new family room look like an integral part of the home's original design.

The full wall of glass, made up of standard sliding glass

doors topped by stationary glass over the header, scoops in abundant light and provides a sweeping view of the delightfully landscaped backyard. Several types of plantings disguise all traces of the former driveway. Colorful annuals brighten one side, and a carefully tended rock garden highlights the slope leading up from the other side. The old driveway itself was covered by new sod.

As the picture *opposite* shows, the interior of the new family room combines rustic, outdoorsy charm with solid, indoor-style comfort. The richly textured fieldstone walls, visible at the far right of the photograph, once had a lime plaster covering that was removed during the early stages of the conversion. Now the walls complement the earth-tone quarry tile floor and pine ceiling.

A basement bonus
Look again at the exterior view *below*. The wooden door beside the patio doors is a new feature, too—it leads to a newly installed second bath and a sauna. (The utility room remains in its original place; the only change necessary was to put up a wall to separate it from the new bath/ sauna area.)

The window above the new door replaced a kitchen door. Formerly, a wooden stairway connected the main level of the house to the backyard; now that there's direct access to the outdoors from both the new family room and the sauna, the old outdoor stairway isn't needed.

The original basement stairs were upgraded to make them safer and more attractive because they're now used regularly to reach the new family room.

AN ABOVEGROUND GARAGE CONVERSION

Most garages aren't tucked under houses—they are attached to the house. For that reason, they're likely to offer light, air, and easy access if and when they are turned into spaces for people. Because attached garages are integral—and often highly noticeable—parts of larger buildings, any architectural changes you make in the process of conversion must be especially well planned.

The greenhouse-style extension pictured *above* provides the finishing touch on a garage-turned-living space. The homeowners had wanted to replace their 20x19-foot garage with a living/dining area plus greenhouse space; they achieved their double goal by bumping the family cars, finishing the garage, and introducing a 16½x5½-foot greenhouse window where the garage doorway had been.

The dressed-up exterior adds to the appearance of the existing house, and the space inside is expansive and welcoming. In all, the owners gained about 400 square feet of living space.

The new room is a split-level family center; its upper level serves as a dining area, visible in the rear of the photograph *at right.* Three steps lead down to the main seating area. A deep, rich shade of green on the walls contrasts with the flood of light coming from the new expanse of glass.

Diagonally laid strip oak flooring tops the original concrete floor. To achieve the bleached look, the oak strips were scrubbed with a diluted solution of white paint, which was followed by two coats of urethane varnish for protection from scuffs and spills. All walls are insulated with rigid foam insulation and finished with drywall.

The greenhouse and the new brick terrace beyond it are visual extensions of the interior remodeling—indeed, of the whole house. Besides adding floor space, the greenhouse windows bring in abundant and much-needed natural light. Constructed of double-hung windows separated by posts 4 feet apart, the greenhouse space is topped by a glass-paneled roof.

A POTPOURRI OF USES

CONNECTING A GARAGE TO A HOUSE

If you have a detached garage and aren't prepared to exchange garage space for living space, consider a garage conversion once removed. In other words, think about connecting the garage to your house and using the new link as extra living space. If you already have a breezeway connecting the house and garage, all the better. Most breezeway connectors are too narrow to serve as rooms in themselves; with the adroit addition of just a little more space, however, a breezeway can make the house-to-garage trafficway an excellent stopping place.

It's difficult to tell where the indoors ends and the out-doors begins in the plant-and-people haven pictured *at right*. Where an open-fronted breezeway once joined the main house to the matching shingled garage, a new breakfast/sun-room now adds valuable living space. The glassed-in area at the front of the breezeway was added—you can see what were exterior or kitchen windows at the left of the photograph.

To double the size of the original breezeway, the owners extended the framework and installed double glazing in the south-facing wall and in the roof. You could achieve much the same effect by adding a new breezeway-style room between a house and a completely detached garage. In that case, you'd have to run utility lines from one structure or the other to the new link, and build framing for the entirely new structure.

In the remodeling project featured here, the existing north wall and roof were beefed up with extra fiberglass insulation, resulting in lower heating bills for the whole house. The top part of the new extended south wall is 1-inch-thick insulating glass; the lower units are operable.

Whether you are converting an existing breezeway or adding one from scratch, plan traffic patterns carefully to avoid interfering with existing paths from house to garage. The simplest course is to arrange furnishings to accommodate through traffic; you might also consider using only a portion of the connecting structure for living space and reserving a gallery to function as a passageway.

A GARAGE
FOR CARS
AND PEOPLE

As we've pointed out in this chapter, when it comes to turning utility areas into living space, a structurally sound, attached garage is a prime candidate. That doesn't necessarily mean relegating the family car to a permanent outdoor life, however; nor does it always mean you have to build a new garage or carport to replace the old one. A compromise conversion that makes room for people yet still leaves room for automobiles may be the ideal solution to your space needs.

Many garages serve as ad hoc potting centers, mudrooms, and toolsheds. The partial garage conversion pictured *at right* does all those jobs full-time—and still has room for a car, as well. The mixed use resulted from building a moderate-size addition to the rear of the garage. Overlooked by and connected to the nearby kitchen, the addition melds garage and living space.

Versatility is the hallmark of this remodeling. One side of the expanded garage includes a laundry, greenhouse, potting area, and storage center—all just a few steps down from the kitchen at the right. The washer and dryer are out of sight in a louvered enclosure visible at the left of the photograph. In front of the laundry center is a wet bar that doubles as a work counter when plants need repotting. New brick floors in all but the car-storage part of the garage are more than good-looking: They also make it easy to clean up spills.

The plant-filled center section of the floor is a recessed oasis cut out of the brick floor. Plants hanging from the cypress rafters are attached to rope pulleys so they can be easily lowered at watering time. A strategically located drain keeps excess water from puddling.

The plants get abundant sunlight from a series of newly installed fixed-glass skylights, and from windows and glass doors (out of camera range) that lead to the backyard patio.

An auxiliary heating system, added after the garage became a multipurpose recreation and entertainment center, keeps the interior warm enough for plants to thrive year-round.

A BASEMENT
TURNED INTO
A FAMILY ROOM

Almost every home needs more family living space—room for informal entertaining, for children to listen to records, for everyone to play board games or watch TV. Most homes also have the potential to provide additional space. It's not always easy, but the opportunity is usually tucked away somewhere. Perhaps the simplest and probably the most popular approach is to annex basement space and turn it into comfortable leisure-time quarters.

Until the owners of the welcoming family room featured here decided to turn underused, below-grade space into a fully used family room, their upstairs living room served in too many roles—from adult conversation center to teenager party spot. Thanks to distinctive design features such as the striking white corner fireplace and natural-wood-raftered ceiling, the new family room is one of the most appealing rooms in the house.

This 16x16-foot room really has two living areas. One is an informal eating area, visible in the foreground of the photograph. The other half of the room is a lounging area with the fireplace as its focal point. The corner fireplace sports a white laminate mantel and exposed metal flue.

To neatly stow all the miscellany that accumulates in a family room, a 9-foot-long storage unit, combining shelves and cupboards, was designed to run along one wall. The closed lower section of the unit houses large serving pieces as well as children's toys and games. Adjustable open shelving in the upper section takes care of books, photographs, accessories, and a small bar.

Once you finish your basement and put up partitions, you're not likely to benefit from heat radiated from a furnace on the other side of a wall. To combat winter and damp-weather chill, these home-owners installed electric baseboard heating units that tuck beneath the storage unit. An air conditioner, partially visible in the upper right corner of the shelving, makes the room comfortable when the weather turns hot.

A BASEMENT REORGANIZED FOR APARTMENT LIVING

Could down-under living be the solution to the space shortage at your house? More than likely, the answer is yes. Most basements, after all, already have walls, floor, and ceiling elements in place, but other challenges still abound. You need to install good lighting, for instance, and eliminate the unsightly clutter of posts, pipes, ducts, and wires native to most basements. The owners of the basement shown here displayed a sculptor's finesse when they incorporated these utilitarian elements into a bright, contemporary apartment.

The sparkling white walls and glossy wood floors of the living room and kitchen pictured here have a chic and welcoming air that has nothing to do with the usual image of a dark, dreary basement. Nevertheless, these two rooms, as well as a bedroom and study, which aren't pictured here, were carved out of what was once an underused area of the home.

To help transform service areas and wasted space, the walls curve, wind, and jog to accommodate wires, pipes, and other evidence of mechanical systems. One exception is in the living/dining area, where exposed heating pipes add high-tech flair and visually link the two rooms.

Lighting for livability

Besides clever camouflaging, generous lighting is a key to the eye appeal and livability of this basement remodeling. In any project of this kind, you need to make the most of any natural light you can bring into a basement. One bonus the owners shrewdly capitalized on is the above-grade window area visible in the photograph *above*. Fluorescent and track lighting further illuminate the scene.

The kitchen pictured *opposite* offers more evidence of the remodelers' creativity. Wall-hugging counter space is supplemented by a curvilinear island that serves as both a storage center and additional work surface. Fluorescent fixtures mounted under the wall cabinets augment the track lighting.

In addition to aesthetics, you must consider safety aspects when planning basement living space: How will you get down there, for example, and what will you do in the event fire breaks out? For more about these, see page 98.

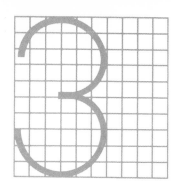
3

IMPROVING STORAGE

No matter how many closets, cabinets, and shelves a home has, its garage, basement, and attic always seem to be called upon to supplement point-of-use storage. Snow tires, bikes, lawn mowers, out-of-season or outgrown clothes—all kinds of house-hold miscellany make their way to one of these spaces. Even if you don't need your basement, garage, or attic for other purposes, you probably feel you could use its storage facilities more efficiently. And if you're planning a conversion of one or more areas, you may be wondering what to do with all the things you used to keep there. Before deciding the only solution to your storage problems is a garage sale, however, take a look at this chapter. It's filled with ideas that prove you can almost always get even more out of—and into—the storage space at your house.

Attics, basements, and garages typically warehouse everything there's no room for elsewhere. Stuff piles up higgledy-piggledy in these zones. Before long you find yourself muttering "I know it's in here *some*where" as you rummage through stacks of items often related only by the times you stored them. When living space overflows into these traditional storage areas, the crunch is likely to become urgent. There's almost always a better way, however.

To determine how to make the best of your storage possibilities, size up the space you have and the items you need to store. Begin by listing everything that requires space—such as patio furniture, tools, and out-of-season clothes.

Once you've identified things that need homes, evaluate their sizes, shapes, and weights. Bulky or heavy objects, such as clothes, sports equipment, snow blowers, and lawn machinery, need different accommodations from what small, light articles require.

Next, determine how much and what type of storage you need. Approximately how many cubic feet of space does each category require? Do you have collections that should be locked up, or gardening chemicals that must be kept out of reach of children? How about boxes of books and accessories that could go on open shelves?

Once you have a fix on these specifics, you're ready to set about converting cluttered space that you've half-ignored over the years into efficient, effective storage places. The following pages explain how.

MAKING CLOSETS WORK HARDER

Closets—whether they directly serve main living areas or are in an attic, basement, or garage—seem to shrink as the years go by. Often one of the best ways to improve storage around any house is to put its closets through some stretching exercises. By modifying a closet to work more efficiently, you can often double or even triple its storage capacity.

Compartmentalize

By having a place for everything, you're more likely to find everything in its place. Custom-tailoring a closet for the items you keep there helps it hold more, and also makes things much more accessible.

For example, the compartmentalized linen closet illustrated *at right* accommodates an entire household's bedding and towels. Because each compartment was especially sized to suit a particular folded linen, you'll never need to rummage through the entire inventory to get fresh towels for an overnight guest or to find a blanket in the middle of a night that suddenly turned cool. The blankets go up top. Niches in the center were tailored especially for bath towels, pillowcases, sheets, and hand towels. Drawers below hold comforters, quilts, and other bulky bedding.

Compartmentalizing makes most sense for items that are highly standardized in size, such as linens, clothing, canned goods, and cleaning supplies. For these, just be sure to leave a few inches of clearance so you can easily get items in and out. However, odd-size gear—such as sports and hobby equipment—might later be supplanted by new acquisitions with slightly or entirely different dimensions. In closets that hold unwieldy

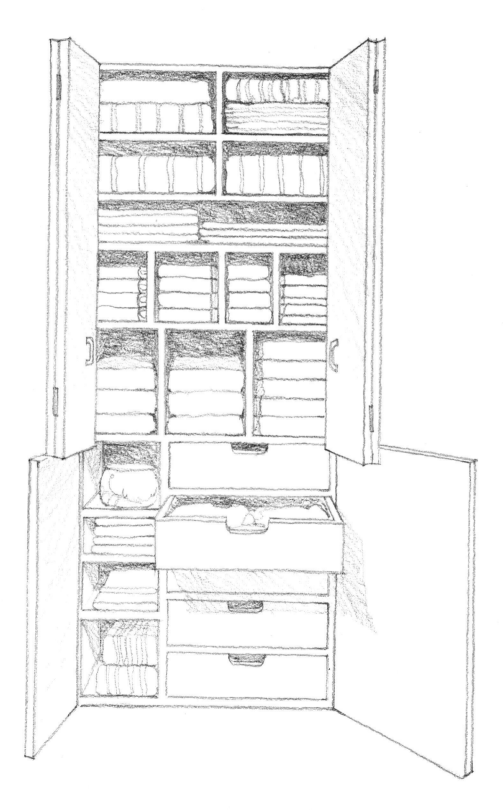

items, install adjustable shelving or compartments that can adapt to changing needs.

Maximize space you have

Originally, the bedroom closet shown *at right* was a typical 2-foot-deep-by-6-foot-wide unit with a pair of sliding doors, a single pole, and a shallow, hard-to-reach top shelf. A modest remodeling changed all that.

First the doors and their frame were removed, along with the soffit above. Up there a sturdy, 2-foot-deep shelf was installed and fronted with lift-up doors to create compartments for suitcases and out-of-season clothes. Below, the closet was divided into three sections. One includes dual-tier rods for shorter garments such as shirts and jackets; in the center, a stack of drawers and open shelves holds socks, underwear, sweaters, and the like; on the far right, a narrow compartment includes a full-height rod for hanging dresses and other longer clothing.

If the closet is for children, hang out-of-season clothes on the top rod, and in-season clothes on the bottom rod where children can reach them. Fill the other half of the closet with stackable storage for games and toys, with seasonal or infrequently used gear on top shelves.

A slightly different arrangement that works equally well is to divide the closet in half vertically, with full-length clothes on one side, shorter clothes on the other, and a bank of drawers or shelves below the shorter clothes.

(continued)

MAKING CLOSETS WORK HARDER
(continued)

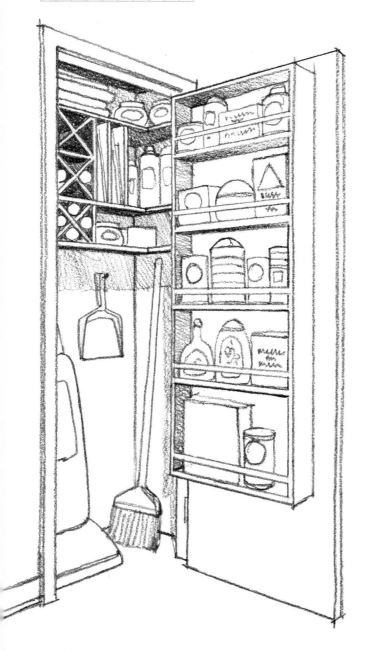

Yet another way to relieve the storage strain at your house is to double or even triple a closet's function. This may mean looking at each storage unit in your home in a different way. An entryway "coat closet," for example, might also be just the place for stereo gear, a bridge table and chairs, or extension leaves for the dining room table.

The versatile closet illustrated *at left* holds down three jobs: It is a utility closet, a wine cellar, and a pantry all rolled into one. Floor space accommodates an upright or canister-model vacuum cleaner, a broom, and a mop. To keep the broom and mop from falling out each time the closet is opened, they're secured to the wall. A dustpan, whisk broom, vacuum cleaner attachments, and often-used household tools hang from hooks on perforated hardboard attached to a side wall.

Above, cubbyholes of various sizes and shapes store everything from bottles of wine to light bulbs to cleaning and polishing supplies. The door on this closet also provides valuable storage space. Shelves attached to its inner face handle grocery overflow from the kitchen.

Adding new closets
No matter how well engineered your existing closets may be, sometimes you simply do not have enough of them. If this is the case at your house, consider adding one. A closet can be built just about anywhere—in a corner, jutting out from a wall, in empty space between studs, even in the middle of a space, as a room divider. Garages, basements, and attics are all prime sites for more closets.

If you have a length of wall that's free, think about using it entirely for storage. A full-wall system is hard to beat because it makes the best use of vertical and horizontal space, and offers more flexibility than any other type of storage.

Wall systems come in all shapes, sizes, and styles. They run the gamut from basic to sophisticated, from a wall of open shelves to a panoply of cabinets, shelves, drawers, bins, racks, and cubbyholes. Before deciding on a wall system, look beyond where you plan to put it and what you plan to use it for. Do you want a stationary wall storage system that's a permanent fixture in a room, or do you want storage you can move to another part of the house or take with you to a new house? A built-in system may be the ideal permanent solution; a freestanding or modular unit makes more sense for temporary arrangements. Easy to install and to move, modular systems offer the most flexibility. You can tailor them to meet a specific need, then rearrange components—or move them to a new location—when your needs change.

The versatile and hardworking wall system illustrated *opposite* meets all of the storage requirements for a basement family center and then some: a wet bar with shelf space for glassware and under-counter space for party accessories and cleaning supplies; a sink to handle cleanup chores; counter space for serving snacks or stacking dirty glasses; and an array of cabinets for games, electronic gear, and books. Even bulky craft and hobby projects are likely to find a home in a storage system this size. So the storage function will not dominate the room, most of it is concealed behind doors.

ORGANIZING STORAGE IN AN UNFINISHED ATTIC

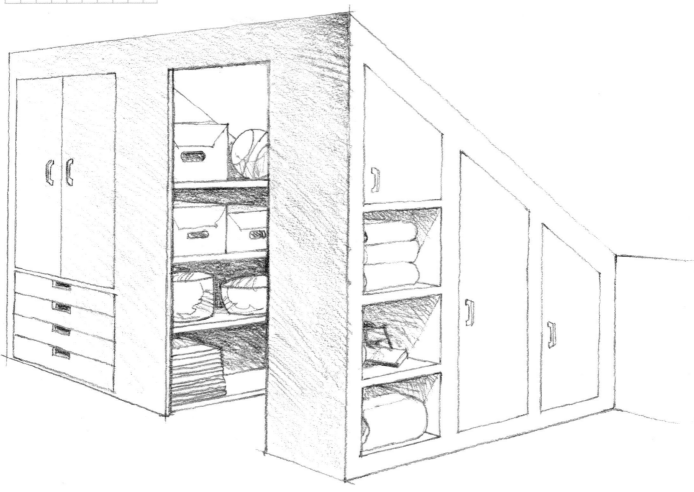

O dd shapes, sharp angles, and limited headroom may rule out finishing an attic for prime living space, but these same architectural features lend themselves well to *semi*-finishing projects. They, in turn, can take a big load off storage facilities elsewhere in your home. Wasted space along the walls under the roofline, for example, offers a storage bonanza. Often so does un-used space at the top of the stairs. To take advantage of these areas without sacrificing valuable space, concentrate on storing up, not out. The two wall storage systems illustrated here do just that.

Organizing your household records
The drawing *opposite* shows a compact unit that works equally well at the head of the stairs or under a sloping roof. If you've ever spent hours leafing through stack after stack of household paperwork to find a misplaced utility bill or insurance policy, you'll ap-preciate the efficiency of this household records organizer.

Two file drawers keep com-pleted business orderly and easy to find. Pullout drawers store office supplies, and ad-justable shelves display books and ledgers. Current bills are filed by due date in a bank of cubbyholes. If you don't need all of the drawer space, re-move some, add a chair and a desk lamp, and you could have a full-scale management center well away from house-hold distractions. To conceal work in progress, close off the unit with a bifold door.

Coping with slopes
Built to fit under a sloping roof, the bounty of open and closed storage units illustrated *above* helps an attic accommodate a wide assortment of articles. In the center is a long, walk-in closet; outside, drawers, shelves, and cabinets stow everything from camping gear to holiday table linens.

If the space under the roof behind an existing kneewall is deep and usable enough, con-sider incorporating it into a storage unit, as well.

Other attic storage possi-bilities include stepped shelving under eaves, shelves or cabinets constructed around doors and windows, and a platform suspended from the ceiling. Overhead platforms work especially well for light-weight, seasonal items, such as blankets or luggage. For a truly tidy, semifinished look, paint storage units and your entire attic with durable semi-gloss paint.

ORGANIZING
GARAGE STORAGE

Hauling a barbecue grill or recreation equipment up and down basement stairs is enough to destroy—or at least lessen—anyone's love of the great outdoors. The answer to problems like these is to make your garage assume a larger share of the backyard storage load.

With today's smaller cars, even a compact garage can accommodate a wide assortment of nonautomotive gear. And because garages have ground-level access to the outdoors, they make an ideal spot to stow things that are used out there.

The illustration *at left* shows one possibility. Here, a garage's rear wall consists of a floor-to-ceiling built-in unit that subtracts only 24 inches from the garage's overall length. Cabinets, bins, a closet, and shelves of varying heights provide plenty of diverse and flexible storage space. (If your garage is unheated, however, store items that could be affected by hot or cold temperatures someplace else.)

Flowerpots, old magazines and newspapers, small hand tools, sports equipment, boating and swimming gear, and outdoor games all store neatly on open shelves. Wire bins work well for bulbs and seeds, garden stakes, small tools, and sports paraphernalia. Cabinets and large bins that lock keep charcoal and grilling accessories, chemicals, building materials, and power tools out of the hands of inquisitive children. If more closed storage is called for, simply substitute cabinets or bins for some of the shelves. A cedar closet provides ample room for out-of-season clothes, but just as easily could house rakes, shovels, and other long

garden tools. Firewood stays dry in an open-front compartment at the base of the unit.

Stealing space for a shop

If your garage has a couple more feet to spare, or you could easily bump out in back, consider incorporating a mini shop for puttering projects, potting plants, or hobby space.

The 4-foot-deep room illustrated and shown in plan view *at left* provides not only work and storage space for household repairs and carpentry projects, but also ample storage for auto, gardening, and recreational needs.

At one end of the room is a stationary workbench, with shelf space below for small projects in progress. Hand tools frequently used are grouped by function and hung from perforated hardboard, so they are easy to find, and equally easy to replace. A fluorescent fixture suspended from the ceiling above the workbench provides task lighting.

Cabinets adjacent to the workbench protect power tools from corrosion, keep containers of nails, screws, and bolts organized, and store paint, solvent, and sandpaper out of sight but within easy reach. Lumber and plywood are stowed overhead, suspended from brackets in the ceiling rafters.

Running the length of the room beyond the shop area is enough storage space to accommodate automobile tires, lawn furniture, gardening tools, sports gear, and plenty more. Cumbersome items, such as bikes, can be suspended from the ceiling or from wall hooks.

Add a passage door between the mini room and the rest of the garage and you can confine noise and dust to the room itself, or leave the entry open for easy access.

INCLUDING STORAGE IN A GARAGE CONVERSION

Turning your garage into a living area often means rethinking your storage needs. With a two-car garage, you have the option of converting only half of the garage to living space. Do this and you'd still have room for one car or lots of equipment.

If you have a small garage, however, other options are in order. For instance, if you don't need shelter for a car, but do want room for the lawn mower, gardening tools, and the like, partition off a small section for them. The most practical place is adjacent to the entry, where you might even be able to use the doors now installed.

Depending on your garage's roofline, its loft area also may offer potential storage space. Items you don't have room for on the remodeled main level can go overhead. Add a pull-down ladder for access to the upper floor.

Inside the new living area, incorporate storage into a special feature, such as a fireplace, a window, or a piece of furniture. In a garage-turned-family center that includes a fireplace, for example, you might decide to add a wall of storage around the fireplace, as illustrated *at right*. Here a prefabricated fireplace unit provides a focal point. Shelves, a cabinet, and roll-out bins flanking the fireplace accommodate everything from firewood to books to a large-size television set. (If you choose to install a fireplace, check local building codes and follow the manufacturer's instructions to the letter.)

Once you decide to convert your garage to living space, what do you do about the garage door—or the gaping hole that used to be the garage door? One solution is to build out 24 inches from the

52

opening and add a glass-roofed storage center like the one shown *at right.* A series of skylights transforms the storage alcove into a bright and airy corner for plants, books, craft and hobby gear, and more. In the evening and on cloudy days, track lights illuminate the area.

Other options include:
• *Retaining the door.* Keep the front section of the garage, door and all, as a storage area for bikes, lawn mowers, and the like. Add storage overhead and along walls. You can even use the back of the garage door for storage; just be sure to leave clearance for opening and closing it.
• *Closing up the door.* If your garage is close to the street, and particularly if the street is a busy one, close up the door and add a storage wall on the street side to muffle noise.
• *Replacing the garage door with a large window.* If the garage has a good view, enclose the door and set in a large window. Wrap storage units around the window.
• *Closing up the door and adding small windows.* To de-emphasize a less-than-perfect view, close up the door but add two or three small windows. Be sure the new windows match others on that side of the house. Add free-standing storage units flush with the wall, or a storage wall or divider closet if the garage is to serve multiple functions.
• *Replacing the garage door with a sliding glass door.* If you don't need an entire wall of storage, consider surrounding a sliding glass door with shelves and closets. Add a privacy fence partway down the old drive, and you could also have a patio.

INCLUDING STORAGE IN A BASEMENT CONVERSION

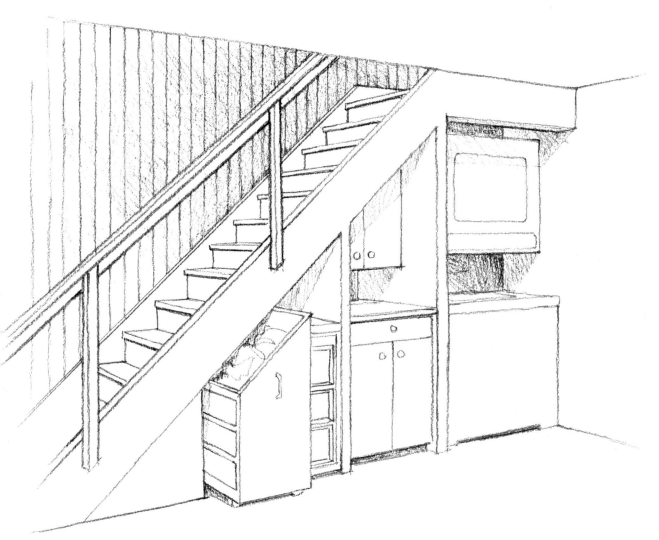

Converting your basement to a family room, home office, or spare bedroom is no bargain if it means giving up valuable storage space. With careful planning, however, you shouldn't have to.

You can, for example, transform one large basement room into two—and gain storage, as well—with a floor-to-ceiling room divider/storage unit like the one illustrated *opposite*. Ideal for a family room, this divider functions as a combination wet bar, entertainment center, and general storage unit. To the right of the sink, shelf space accommodates glassware, bar gear, and a stereo receiver. Below, cabinets encase additional bar accessories, board games, and reading materials.

As the floor plan *opposite* indicates, space on one side of the divider serves as a sitting area, space on the other as a game room. A pass-through simplifies shared use of the areas. For added convenience, you might want to substitute a small refrigerator for some of the cabinets.

Clean living

For basement storage that's convenient but out of the mainstream of family living, consider space under and alongside the basement stairs.

If plumbing permits, you could put a laundry center under the stairway. Stack a washer and dryer, as illustrated *above,* and fill the adjacent area with counter space, drawers, a roll-out hamper, and cabinets and adjustable shelves for detergents, bleach, and softeners. You also could install side-by-side machines, with shelf and cabinet space above. If there's room, add a fold-down ironing board and even a mini sewing center.

If relocating your laundry under the basement stairs is impractical, use the space for a collection of roll-out locker-type storage units for sports and recreational equipment, out-of-season clothes, and luggage. Or add cabinets and shelves to accommodate a pantry, wine cellar, or hobby center. Close off the entire under-stair area with a bifold door to keep projects and storage out of sight.

For additional storage space in the stair area, consider narrow shelves or hooks on the walls along the stairway, and platforms suspended from the stairway ceiling.

If you've exhausted storage space up top and down under, you may find a solution out back. Adding on to your house or garage or building a separate structure is a good way to provide safe, year-round storage for all sorts of seasonal paraphernalia.

Although backyard storage possibilities abound, the trick is to choose storage that's good-looking, hardworking, *and* unobtrusive. The garden shed illustrated *above* is all three. Incorporated into a patio scheme, it's rugged and attractive, and nearly disappears into the privacy fence surrounding the patio.

A single large compartment provides enough room for patio furniture and accessories, lawn and gardening equipment, barbecue gear, and almost anything else you might want to store there. The extra-wide entry makes it easy to get bulky items in and out. Tucking trash cans into the side of the shed keeps them upright and safe from marauding animals. Clippers, hedge trimmers, lawn and garden chemicals, and the like are stowed behind a locked door, where they're safely out of reach of children.

The storage bank pictured *opposite* nestles along one side of a garage, under the eaves, providing another practical hideaway for outdoor storage. Separate compartments allow items to be grouped and stored by function: furniture and outdoor entertaining gear in one receptacle, lawn and garden equipment in another, barbecue and grilling accessories in another, and recreational equipment in still another. The number of storage compartments you elect to incorporate into such an addition depends on what and how much you have to store.

Outdoor storage possibilities are almost limitless. Other options include building storage under the floors of a deck or a gazebo, adding storage space to a children's playhouse or a greenhouse,

and incorporating storage features into patio and deck furniture.

General considerations

When you add storage space to a house or garage, be sure it's compatible with the style and appearance of the rest of the house. One of the advantages detached storage has over attached storage is that it often is easier to screen. If storage space is attached to a house or garage, consider installing a connecting door. This would be a real blessing in wet weather, should you want to move items from one spot to another.

Before you do any building or adding on, however, be sure to check local zoning regulations and requirements. Many communities require building permits before construction can begin. Some also specify whether and where you can build a storage structure on your property.

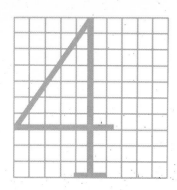

PLANNING BONUS SPACES

Most houses have hidden treasure spaces in the form of a basement, attic, or garage. They often—and sometimes easily—can become living space. In Chapter 2, we showed you how 10 families turned previously underused areas into highly livable additions to their homes. Before you can begin to claim a bonus space at your house, though, you'll need to do some careful planning. This chapter tells you what kinds of things you'll need to know or think about before you knock down the first wall, repair the first floor, or strengthen the first joist.

SIZING UP BONUS SPACES

Look closely—very closely—and possibly you can tell that the meticulously appointed family room pictured *opposite* was once a garage. Where the door used to be, a multipaned picture window now bathes the room in pleasant natural light. For a cozy country look, the owners covered the concrete floor with random-plank flooring, added a beamed ceiling, and installed a fireplace. The result: a warm, charming room in what once were utilitarian surroundings.

If you'd like to achieve this kind of makeover magic in a presently unfinished space at your house, think about all the possibilities before you tackle the down-to-earth details of planning and executing the transformation.

Inspiration and discovery

You may have a garage, basement, *and* attic at your house; yet, only one of them probably stands out as the best possible candidate for an all-out conversion. As you think about the three zones, consider not only which one you can spare most readily, but also how best to use each.

• *Basement.* Look down, and you'll find what may be an ideally isolated area. Far from the madding crowd above, the basement is often a perfect spot for getting away from it all. A home office or study is a splendid choice for such silent surroundings. And for different reasons, a basement is ideal, almost as is, as a multipurpose workshop. There, family members can drill, saw, hammer, and bang to their hearts' content without disturbing other people.

You can also convert a basement into a traditional, full-fledged family room; an adults-only entertainment center; a

bedroom for an older child or a relative who is now part of the household; or even an imaginative mixture of different areas for different uses. One example: a combination laundry and exercise room.

• *Attic.* Many attics have the potential to go from dark, dusty, uninviting hideaways to airy, light-filled, thoroughly enjoyable living spaces. Although most have certain built-in limitations—they're not the greatest party rooms, for instance—attics are nevertheless top locations for one or more bedrooms, a study, a quiet workroom or sanctuary for a hobbyist, a playroom, or even a family-only retreat, complete with a cozy wood stove or fireplace.

• *Garage.* Among the most utilitarian of structures, sheltering one or two cars and an abundance of odds and ends, a garage (and with some modification, a carport, too) is also one of the most versatile bonus spaces you'll find. For example, it's usually close to the kitchen, so it's a convenient location for a new family room.

In addition, a pint-size, two-bedroom house with an attached garage can quickly gain a third sleeping space. Again, because kitchen plumbing is often nearby, it might make economic sense to add a bathroom as well.

If you do business from your home, converting a garage into an office or studio might also be a compelling option (assuming, of course, that local ordinances allow it). Not only does this change of space provide welcome privacy, it also permits you to meet with clients and associates without disturbing the rest of the family. *(continued)*

SIZING UP
BONUS SPACES
(continued)

How you use bonus spaces ultimately depends on your style of living. What's important to you and your family? What are you unable to do now—or unable to do comfortably—that you *could* do in revamped surroundings? The three examples on these two pages show how different families recaptured space and made it work usefully for them.

Up and at 'em

The owners of one home, faced with an unused 1,200-square-foot attic, decided to take advantage of that space in a number of ways. They divided it into several rooms: a master bedroom and bath, an office for the work-at-home husband, a guest bedroom, and a sewing center, shown *at left*, for the wife, who spends many hours there working on projects and conducting classes. The home office is visible behind the cutting table, against the wall, and the guest bedroom is on the other side.

Creating an almost sculpturelike effect, the owners relied on existing dormer lines to design the ceilings. White and pale blue walls reflect light extraordinarily well, a key point in the remodeling because the owners also decided to remove the roof at the ridge line, replacing it with a 28-foot-long, 4-foot-wide skylight that illuminates what had been a dark and dreary area. Finally, the durable, easy-to-clean marble floor is a natural for this now heavily traveled living area.

Downstairs delights

Another pair of owners looked down, to an unfinished, 1,000-square-foot walkout basement in their traditional two-story home. Their object was to fashion an integrated space for both indoor and outdoor entertaining. They got it by adding a kitchen, bar, bathroom, and storage area in one half and using the other to build a multipurpose room, pictured *at upper right*. Doors in this room lead out to a new deck, patio, and backyard tennis court.

The center of attention is the room's media appeal. Bifold doors open to reveal a large-screen television set and close when the TV is unused. The projector is housed in a custom-made laminate table in front of the screen, and wiring for all the electronic equipment is conveniently tucked behind the storage space.

From the start, two things made this particular basement a logical candidate for finishing school. First, it's a walkout, providing not only access to the outside, but also natural light in an area where it's often hard to come by. Second, it has 10-foot-high ceilings, so too little headroom was never a problem.

Shaping up

Squeezing the most out of meager space is a challenge many homeowners face when converting a basement. Combine and conquer is the solution one family chose, and the winning results are evident *at lower right*.

This brightly colored area works hard in three different ways. One, it's a laundry room, complete with built-in storage, which mini-slat blinds hide from view when necessary. Two, it's a retreat for the home computer buff. And three, it's an exercise room complete with rubber-mat flooring. Not shown are a storage center for the exercise equipment and an in-the-wall stereo system.

PUTTING CHANGES ON PAPER

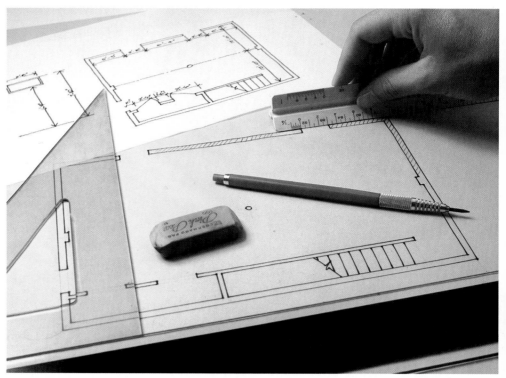

Once you have a mental image of a useful and attractive, finished-off bonus space, it's time to devise a precise plan for the room. Don't shy away from doing this paperwork; it's painstaking, but it's neither time-consuming nor difficult—especially when you consider the time and materials wasted if you set out without a plan and make a big mistake.

Begin with the tools shown *above:* a measuring tape, a sharp pencil and eraser (the architect's pencil pictured here is a luxury, not a necessity), graph paper, tracing paper,

masking tape, a clear triangle, an architect's scale and template, a felt-tip marker, and a T-square.

First do a freehand sketch of the area. Forget, for the moment, about perfect proportions and straight lines. Instead, concentrate on rough shapes, noting the positions of

doors, windows, and other fixed elements.

Next, start measuring—very carefully—as shown *opposite, bottom left.* Determine the width and depth of door and window openings, along with the distances between them. Also note the direction doors swing, the position of stair-wells, and the distances between any other fixtures. While you're working, write each measurement on the sketch, and then double-check to make sure it's accurate.

Finally, do a scaled drawing (¼ inch per foot) of the area. Tape a piece of tracing paper over graph paper divided into ¼-inch squares, and neatly draw the room. Rely on the architect's scale to check graph-paper counts.

Now the fun begins: your opportunity to experiment—free of charge—with as many potential layouts as you can think of, testing the location of a closet here, the position of a partition there. Tape another piece of tracing paper over the finished "before" drawing, and rough-in scaled possibilities for the room, erasing as necessary and using as much tracing paper as you like.

Once you have the floor plan you like, cut out scaled templates of the furnishings, equipment, appliances, and other items you'll place in the space. Move them around until you arrive at a workable, comfortable arrangement, as shown *at upper right.* Again, feel free to change the drawing if you need to.

The final step is to make a finished, scaled drawing of the area as you want it to be. If your plan includes complicated changes, you may want a pro to do it for you; otherwise, use the same tools as before to complete a drawing similar to the one *at lower right.*

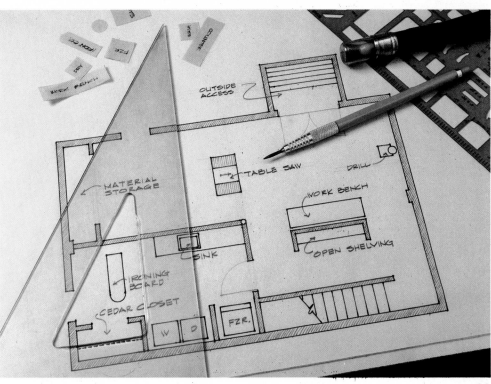

PLANNING A FAMILY ROOM IN THE GARAGE

The photograph *at right* shows a finished plan for converting the two-car garage pictured *above* into a full-service family room. Rather than specifying a walled-off opening to replace the garage door, as many conversions do, this plan calls for a large bay window. This change will provide welcome light and solar warmth, serve as an eye-appealing architectural feature on the outside, and create room for a window seat inside.

The plan goes a long way toward eliminating the odd-room-out, unintegrated feeling common to many converted garages. Minor changes—closing up the original door to the house, creating a wide opening to the kitchen, and adding a new step to a quarry-tile floor in front of a wet bar—clearly signal that this is the family room, part of the house but distinct from other areas in it. A much bigger change, adding sliding glass doors and a deck off the rear, helps extend the scope of the room by bringing the indoors out and the outdoors in.

On the wall farthest from the house, the plan calls for a new, heat-efficient fireplace, flanked by built-ins for entertainment gear and a desk.

(continued)

GARAGE CONVERSION TIPS

If you've decided to convert your garage to living space, keep the following points in mind as you plan. See pages 84-87 for more about these.

• Most garages are framed with wall studs that are 7 feet high—too low for a typical ceiling. Common solutions are installing a suspended ceiling or building a cathedral ceiling.

• To heat a garage, you often have two options—add to existing ductwork or use a separately controlled self-contained source of heat. Determine, too, whether you can extend existing wiring and whether plumbing can go in at an affordable cost.

• A garage's boxy interior can be a design problem. Small structural changes, such as removing part of a wall, help.

• You probably won't want a concrete floor. Before covering it, repair damaged sections and level the floor.

• As with any major remodeling job, check building codes early. Most, for example, stipulate that a wall between the garage and living space be more fire resistant than an ordinary partition, something to remember if you're thinking of converting half of a two-car garage.

GIMLET/GIBSON BAR SINKS

Convenient and colorful.
Durable acrylic, resists chipping and staining.
Self-rimming for neater, quicker installation.
Continental-styled faucet.

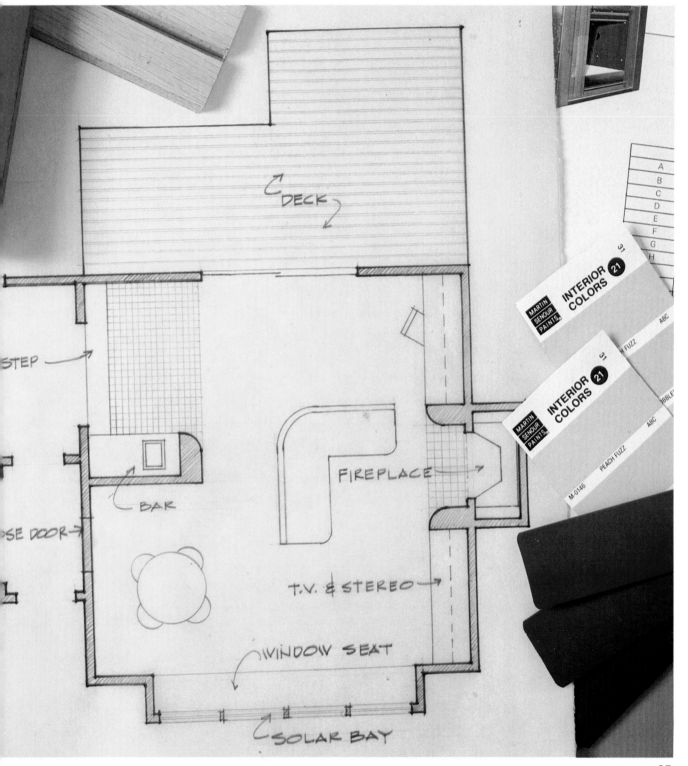

STEP

DECK

BAR

SE DOOR

FIREPLACE

T.V. & STEREO

WINDOW SEAT

SOLAR BAY

MARTIN SENOUR PAINTS
INTERIOR COLORS 21
31

MARTIN SENOUR PAINTS
INTERIOR COLORS 21
31

PEACH FUZZ

M-0146   PEACH FUZZ

A
B
C
D
E
F
G
H

65

PLANNING A FAMILY ROOM IN THE GARAGE
(continued)

Garages are by nature boxy. To help combat that, our conversion plan introduces curves—to one side of the wet bar, on each side of the fireplace, and in the L-shaped seating unit. Vertical wood paneling dresses up these and other surfaces.

The wet bar, because it's adjacent to the original house, easily taps into existing plumbing. Cabinets, drawers, and glass shelving here help keep bar supplies organized. The quarry tile floor takes everyday spills in stride.

Because no house ever seems to have enough storage and work space, we included nearly an entire wall of cabinetry on both sides of the fireplace and more under the bumped-out window seat. The fireplace itself is a prefabricated, heat-circulating unit. Not shown in this view are the sliding glass doors that open to the new deck out back. These put outdoor living and dining space just a few feet from the kitchen.

PLANNING A
TOTAL WORK AREA
IN THE BASEMENT

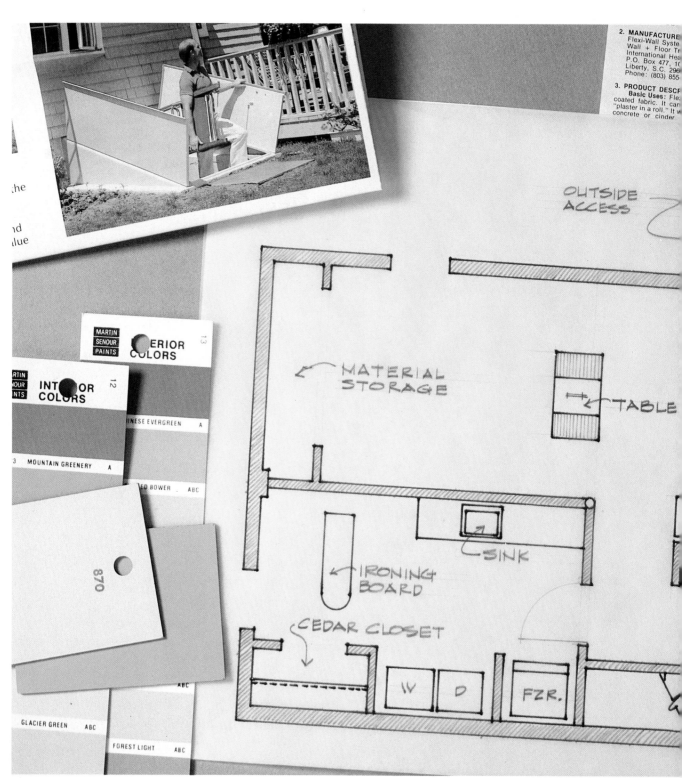

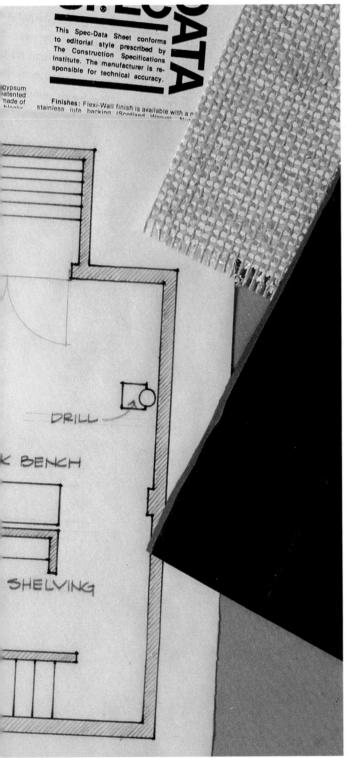

Take one humdrum basement (part of which is shown *above*), plan carefully, and you've got a hardworking layout similar to the one shown *at left*. It's both a handyperson's haven and a laundry area, with plenty of storage and room for a built-in freezer.

Key to the planned workshop is the location of the bench and power tools (here's where scaled templates come in handy); there's more than enough room to maneuver big pieces of lumber and to move easily from station to station. Just as important, a set of wide stairs leading outside serves both as access to the backyard and as a convenient portal for moving materials in and out. At the other end of the workshop is a half-wall of partially enclosed storage space; freestanding open shelving adjacent to the workbench supplements this.

The laundry room is partitioned off from the work space. Here a washer, dryer, ironing board, and sink are arranged in an easy-to-work-in triangle similar to the one in the shop. A large cedar closet stores all types of clothing. Placing the freezer just inside the door and not far from the main stairwell makes access to it possible without going through the workshop or the laundry room.   *(continued)*

BASEMENT CONVERSION TIPS

Usually, basement heating, wiring, and plumbing systems are already in place, and access is often not a problem. Even so, you need to address certain points of order when planning a downstairs conversion. (See pages 76-79 for more about this.)

• A fact of life in many basements is lack of headroom. If your ceiling is lower than 7 feet, plan on dropping the floor level enough to make the space usable. That's a difficult job—digging by hand, for the most part—but you can do it if you have the time and a strong back (or if you pay someone else to do the work). In either case, get the advice of an experienced masonry contractor first.

• Basements are notorious leakers, and part of finishing them off is drying them out. A new, insulated interior wall will cure condensation problems, and two coats of waterproofing masonry paint can stop moisture from seeping through the walls. For more wet-basement solutions, see pages 148 and 149.

• Ceilings are another priority. Acoustic tiles take up little space. Suspended ceilings may drop down too far. Drywall usually requires a professional's touch.

PLANNING A TOTAL WORK AREA IN THE BASEMENT
(continued)

Welcome to a functional yet attractive underground room. This illustration demonstrates how effectively the space could function as two thoughtfully separated work areas.

Unlike the garage-turned-family room shown earlier, where walls were removed, the major change here comes from partitions that separate the home workshop from the laundry room.

The materials chosen for new partitions have a lot to do with the appearance of a proposed conversion. Here, a simple, easy-care surface, such as drywall, makes sense. In a space intended for neater pursuits, you might choose paneling or other decorative material.

Note, too, how careful placement of the workbench, open shelving, and table saw makes it easy to move around in what could have been close quarters. In a shop—especially one where you might be working with paints, varnishes, and other fume-producers—be sure to provide adequate ventilation. One easy way to do that is to replace part of a basement window with an exhaust fan.

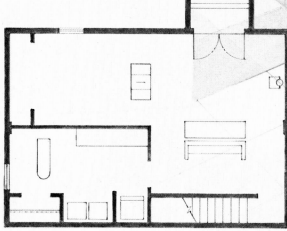

PLANNING A SLEEPING RETREAT IN THE ATTIC

The attic pictured *above* has lots of potential, but little else. The plan shown *at right* turns it into a complete living area for older children or teenagers.

This design takes advantage of an attic's best potential features—natural light and good ventilation—in a couple of ways: It adds a pair of windows and a strategically placed operable skylight. Both will provide sunlight, moonlight, and pleasant cross-ventilation to the bedroom and study area, which is raised on a platform two steps above the attic floor.

Kneewalls on each side close off dead zones under the eaves. Where the kneewalls end, however, abundant space for hanging clothes begins. On the other side of the staircase, which divides the attic into two equal-size areas, are partitions enclosing a storage room and new bath. Though small, the bath is complete, with a vanity-style lavatory, toilet, and shower.

The plan also solves a major systematic question in a straightforward way. Rather than extend existing ductwork and tie into the main furnace, it calls for a new self-contained furnace, sized to warm only the rooms it has to and hidden away behind a new door.

(continued)

ATTIC CONVERSION TIPS

Like basements and garages, attics have their own planning points you need to be aware of before getting down to the actual work (see pages 80-83).

• Headroom is high on the list. If your attic doesn't have it, look elsewhere for bonus space. Ordinarily, 10 feet, measured from the attic floor to the ridge beam, is a minimum.

• Access is just as important. An existing stairway with sufficient headroom solves the problem. If you hope to put in a new stairway, keep a few points in mind. On the floor below, you'll have to allow at least a 3x10-foot rectangle for a conventional stairway or a 5½-foot square for circular stairs. In the area above the staircase, headroom should be at least 78 inches from step to roof at any point along the rise. Usually, this means positioning stairs immediately below the roof ridge or parallel to the roof's slope.

• Attic joists often need strengthening before you can put in a finished floor. Have an architect or building contractor check yours (see pages 154 and 155).

• Determine early how you can most efficiently extend heating, plumbing, and electrical service. (See Chapter 9.)

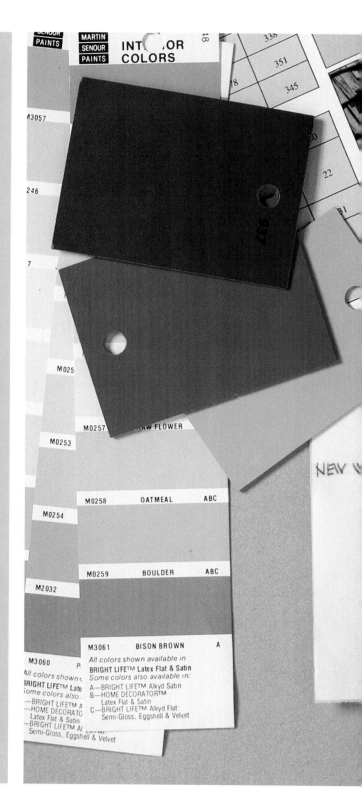

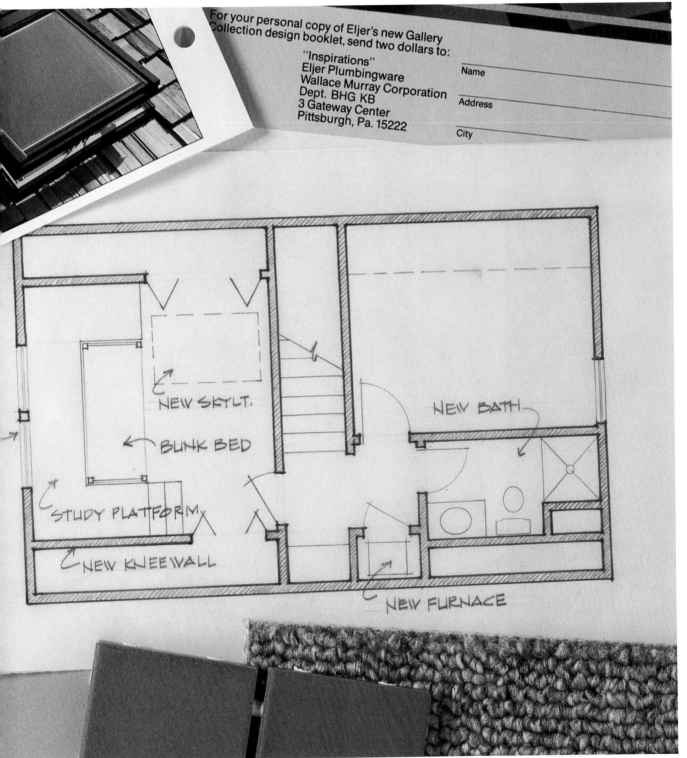

For your personal copy of Eljer's new Gallery
Collection design booklet, send two dollars to:

"Inspirations"
Eljer Plumbingware
Wallace Murray Corporation
Dept. BHG KB
3 Gateway Center
Pittsburgh, Pa. 15222

Name

Address

City

NEW SKYLT.

BUNK BED

STUDY PLATFORM

NEW KNEEWALL

NEW BATH

NEW FURNACE

PLANNING A SLEEPING RETREAT IN THE ATTIC
(continued)

This illustration gives you a look at our attic plan from inside the door leading to the sleeping and study area.

It's easy to see that headroom is no problem here, and the design makes full use of available space. The ceiling follows the existing rafter line, and windows fill the generous expanses of vertical wall space at gable ends.

An operable skylight provides an additional and dramatic source of light. Installing one is a project that a moderately skilled do-it-yourselfer could accomplish. Most manufacturers include step-by-step instructions (for more about skylights, see pages 118 and 119).

The illustration also points up another neat twist to this design: The platform bed is accessible from both the original floor and the raised level. The resulting gallery effect adds special appeal to this recycled space.

Our plan is for a children's room. For adult sleeping quarters, you might want to raise only the bed, and perhaps a couple of end tables.

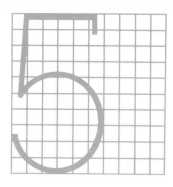

GETTING THE SPACE READY

Compared to adding on, converting an unfinished garage, basement, or attic into living space is relatively easy. The elements already in place—the walls, the roof, and the floor—serve as solid foundations for new surfaces. Preparing these backdrops for their new roles takes a good deal less time, effort, and expense than building from scratch. In this chapter, we'll take you through the preliminary steps required to turn utilitarian spaces into warm, inviting, and comfortable rooms.

Because basements are essentially unfinished rooms, you'll be dealing for the most part with adding a new surface, such as drywall or paneling.

Before putting up new walls, however, you'll want to "fur out" the old ones with inexpensive 1x2s or 1x3s or with a 2x4 framework. Using 2x4s leaves more room for pipes, insulation, and electrical wiring, but cuts down on floor space. For walls that are even to begin with, 1x2 furring strips will do. Use construction glue or masonry nails to attach furring strips flat side down. If you use nails, aim for the mortar joints between the blocks.

Use standard 16-inch center-to-center spacing for vertical furring. Doing so eliminates a lot of trimming of standard 4-foot-wide sheets of drywall or paneling. Use a level or chalk line to make

sure floor-to-ceiling strips are plumb and centered before attaching them to the concrete block wall. Nail horizontal furring strips at the ceiling and floor and fit short pieces around windows and doors.

To avoid disturbing your new work, make sure all your new electrical wiring, switches, outlets, and fixtures are already in place before you put up the furring.

If your basement walls are not perfectly plumb, or if their surfaces are very uneven, you may well want to build a standard 2x4 stud wall, shimmed from behind to make the new wall flat. First, nail a 2x4 top plate to the basement's ceiling joists and a soleplate to the concrete floor. Then, toenail 2x4 studs to both plates, spaced and centered at 24-inch intervals. Finally, apply the drywall or paneling.

(continued)

IN THE
BASEMENT
(continued)

No matter how attractive your basement may become, it will not be inviting unless it's also physically comfortable all year long. For temperature control and heating and cooling efficiency, that means insulation.

Depending upon where you live and how much space you're willing to sacrifice for insulation, you have two choices: rigid foam panels and planks or soft batts and blankets. If you use the rigid variety, you can glue them to the wall or wedge them between 1x2 furring; the batts and blankets are thicker, and require a 2x3 or 2x4 stud wall over the masonry. In either case, let the insulation's R-value be your guide. Soft insulation usually has a rating of about R-3 per inch of thickness. Foam ranges from R-4 to R-8 per inch. In mild-winter areas, an R-7 rating will do. In colder regions, go for an R-11.

Because rigid foam insulation is highly combustible, you must cover it with a minimum of ½ inch of drywall, even if you plan to finish the wall with paneling. Drywall, also called gypsum wallboard, is a dense, durable, noncombustible material. It comes in 4x8-foot panels that are ⅜, ½, or ⅝ inch thick. Most building codes specify ½-inch drywall for home construction, but if you'll be attaching drywall to ¾-inch-thick furring, get ⅝-inch panels; you'll need the extra ⅛ inch so nails won't hit masonry behind the furring.

You can make most straight cuts in drywall panels with a heavy-duty utility knife and a straightedge. Measure and mark your cut first. Align the straightedge, score through the paper covering, snap the panel along the scored line, and slice through the paper backing to separate the sections.

You can glue rigid foam insulation to the wall or wedge it between furring strips. With a utility knife, trim the panels to fit, run several beads of construction adhesive along the back side, and press into place. Where winters are severe, you may need blanket or batt insulation that will require a 2x4 stud wall over the masonry.

With rigid foam insulation, use plastic sheeting as a vapor barrier. Staple it to the furring strips with a tacker that can handle ³⁄₁₆-, ¼-, or ⅝-inch staples (so you can use it for other projects). Press the base of the tacker against the surface and push on the lever. Pull the plastic tight as you go and be generous with the staples, spacing them only a few inches apart.

As durable as it is, drywall is still easy to cut. To accommodate electrical outlets, measure and mark their position on the drywall, drill holes at each corner, and cut the opening with a keyhole saw. After you've cut each panel to fit, run several beads of construction adhesive along the back side, and press into place.

To hide drywall seams, apply premixed compound to the tapered trough between panels. While the compound is still wet, press a length of paper tape along the same path using the 4-inch knife. After it dries, apply another coat of compound. Sand or sponge lightly to smooth. Then, apply a finishing coat of compound and sand or sponge again to complete the job.

Installing drywall

You can install the panels vertically or horizontally. Choose the arrangement that minimizes the number of joints you'll have to patch and fill later. Nail the panels to the furring strips or studs with 1¼-inch ring-shank drywall nails. You'll need about 5½ pounds of nails for every 1,000 square feet of wall surface.

Space the nails about 8 inches apart along the furring strips. Drive them in with enough force to "dimple" the nailheads just below the surface of the drywall, but try not to break the panel's paper covering.

Once the drywall is in place, you'll need to camouflage the joints and nailheads. This multistep process will require lots of time and about three gallons of premixed joint compound and 250 feet of paper tape for each 500 square feet of wall surface.

While you're at it, invest in a pair of 4- and 10-inch-wide finishing knives. For the joints, use the 4-inch knife to apply a swath of compound to the tapered trough between panels. Then, apply a length of paper tape along the same path. Let the taped joint dry for about 24 hours, then apply another coat of compound, feathering out the edges about 6 inches. When the second coat is dry, smooth it out by sanding lightly or wiping with a damp sponge, but don't expose the paper tape again.

Finally, apply a skim coat of compound with the 10-inch knife, feathering the edges out 5 or 6 inches on each side of the center. Sand or sponge smooth again. Fill nail dimples and other surface imperfections the same way, but omit the tape.

Like a basement, an unfinished attic is a room in waiting. There are a few caveats to keep in mind, however. If your plans call for an attic-level bathroom, try to position it above the downstairs bath (or laundry room or kitchen) to make extending the water-supply lines and drains easier and more economical. Before you get down to making walls, floors, and ceilings in the attic, put in the plumbing, heating and air-conditioning ducts, and wiring.

Insulation needs

Once the mechanical work is out of the way, the pace of conversion picks up. The next step is to insulate the new room so it will be comfortable year-round. How much insulation you'll need depends on where you live, of course, but generally, it's better to over-insulate than to underinsulate. Cut corners here and you'll pay for it in the form of higher energy bills. Check with your local building department for recommendations for your area.

As for the type of insulation, you can choose fiberglass or rock-wool batts, which come in easy-to-handle sections 4 to 8 feet long; blankets, which come in continuous rolls you cut to size; or bagged loose-fill. For most attic projects you'll probably want to use at least two of the three—loose-fill for the floor, and batts or blankets for walls and ceilings.

Loose-fill insulation is often the insulation of choice for attic floors because in bagged form it's easy to handle and install and because it fills in irregular spaces. All you have to do is pour out the desired depth between joists.

Mineral-wool and fiberglass insulation are harmful to lungs, skin, and eyes, so dress for the occasion with a painter's mask, goggles, gloves, and long sleeves. If you use bagged loose-fill insulation, pour it in to fill every nook and cranny but don't pack it down. Lay a board across joists and drag it back and forth to level the insulation.

With 2x4 kneewalls, studs are first nailed between top plate and soleplate. Then each of the plates is nailed to roof rafters and floor joists. Note that you'll have to cut the tops of studs to conform to the angle of your roof's pitch.

Be sure, however, to keep loose-fill and other insulators at least 3 inches away from recessed light fixtures. Covering or crowding them could cause a fire. Install wood barriers between joists on each side of a fixture to keep the insulation in place. To make your job easier, take some planks or pieces of plywood into the attic before you start. This will give you something solid to kneel on as you work.

Building walls

Hold off on other attic insulation projects until you've framed in your room-to-be, converting part of the roof's sloping surface into vertical walls. Called kneewalls because they're usually only 4 to 5 feet high, they're really just attic adaptations of the standard stud wall.

The work will go faster if you frame kneewalls on the floor and then raise them into position. You'll need a soleplate at the bottom, a top plate where the new wall meets the rafters, and a series of vertical studs, all of them made from standard 2x4s, centered at 24-inch intervals.

Measure, mark, and cut all the components first. Lay them out on a temporary plywood floor. Use two 10-penny nails to nail through the soleplate into the studs. Use two more to nail through the top plate into the studs. When the kneewall is assembled, stand it up, position it between floor and roof (use a plumb line to make sure it's perfectly vertical), and then nail the top plate to the rafters and the bottom plate to the floor joists.

(continued)

Installing a new subfloor in your attic takes less time than you might think. Because you'll be working with 4x8-foot sheets of plywood or particleboard, the job goes fairly quickly. But, as with other remodeling projects, preparation is crucial, and you must consider several key factors.

First, if the joists are made of lumber smaller than 2x8s you'll have to reinforce them. To do so, cut new joists of the same size and length, and nail them to the 2x4 plates at each end and to the sides of the existing joists at regular intervals. If the old joists are spaced more than 16 inches apart, add new ones between them for extra support. For more about sizing joists, see pages 154 and 155.

Next comes the subfloor, usually sheets of ⅝-inch Grade C-D plywood (with the C side facing up) or ⅝-inch particleboard. Before cutting and nailing it to the joists, work out an arrangement that will avoid aligning joints along the same joists. To do this, stagger the sheets in a long-short, short-long way so the end of one sheet is not aligned with the end of the one right next to it. This method will make the floor stronger and less squeak-prone. To allow for expansion and contraction of the wood and to prevent buckling, leave ⅛-inch spaces between the sides of the sheets and 1/16-inch spaces between the ends.

Nail panels to each of the joists, spacing coated No. 8 nails about 6 inches apart and staggering them at joints to prevent splitting the joist below. Underlayment made of ¼-inch hardboard in 4x8-foot

You can use board lumber to build a subfloor, but ⅝-inch plywood or particleboard is easier, faster, and stronger. Topped with a layer of ¼-inch hardboard underlayment, it provides a durable yet resilient foundation for tile, carpet, or wood flooring. A strong subfloor also gives you something to stand on while working on other projects.

Cut batt or blanket insulation strips to fit snugly between the studs of the kneewalls and the rafters of the roof. If the insulation has a built-in vapor barrier, make sure it faces into the room. Find out from your local building department the R-value recommended for home use in your part of the country.

A heavy-duty staple tacker makes putting up batts or blankets of insulation an easy chore. Because you can use the tool with one hand, you can hold the insulation in place with the other. If the insulation has a vapor barrier, staple it to the studs' room-side edges; if it does not, staple it to the sides of studs as shown.

Polyethylene sheeting not only provides an effective vapor barrier (for use with insulation that doesn't already have one), but also cuts down on air infiltration, which can rob you of expensive heated or cooled air. Pull the sheeting tight and use a staple tacker to fasten it to the edges of studs and rafters.

sheets goes on top of the subflooring, but perpendicular to it in order to smooth over the joints. Again, stagger the pattern of the hardboard as you did the subflooring. Space the sheets apart by about 1/32 inch and keep them 1/8 inch out from the walls. Use No. 8 box nails again or special underlayment nails to fasten the underlayment (rough side up) to the subflooring (but not to the joists themselves).

Now your new subfloor is ready for tile, carpeting, or tongue-and-groove wood flooring. To avoid marring the final surface, don't install it until you've completed all heavy-duty construction work.

Insulating attic walls and ceilings

Cut and install batt or blanket insulation between the studs of the gable walls and the new kneewalls and between the roof rafters. Both kinds of insulation come with paper covers (one side may be a vapor barrier, which should face into the room) and a reinforced paper flange along each side so you can staple the insulation to studs and rafters. Space the staples only 3 or 4 inches apart.

If you select a soft insulation that has no built-in vapor barrier, create one by covering the insulated walls and ceiling with 4-mil polyethylene sheeting, pulled tight and stapled to rafters and studs. A plastic vapor barrier keeps the insulation dry and also creates an effective additional barrier to air infiltration.

Putting drywall on a garage ceiling is not a one-person job. But a T brace—made from a 2x4 stud topped with a 1x4 cross member—can help once you and your assistant properly position the drywall. Make the brace the same height as the ceiling, minus the thickness of the drywall.

Before surfacing the walls with drywall or paneling, bring your new room's electrical system up to par by adding additional outlets, switches, and fixtures. Use a spade bit to drill holes in the studs to make a path for electrical cables. Because your work may need a local building inspector's approval, make sure you follow the building codes.

Except for its concrete floor, nothing resembles a conventional room addition more closely than an attached garage does. Again, because the major construction work has already been done, a fill-in-the-blanks strategy is all that's required to convert unfinished space to a valuable living area. Once the garage door has been removed and replaced with a solid wall—or windows—you have a room in the raw, requiring only the finishing touches.

Before you start, analyze your family's needs and wants, and consider the opportunities the space offers. To make the room light and bright you may want to enlarge or add to the windows already in place. Or how about sliding glass doors where the garage door once was? Before drywall goes up you have the chance to incorporate these and other features. Don't automatically write off the garage's upper level, either. It may offer ample storage possibilities, so consider flooring it with plywood and providing a stairway for easy access. And what about the fireplace you've always wanted? Freestanding or built-in, now is the time to work it into your plans and budget.

Speaking of budget, one major expenditure you may want to consider is installing a new floor to match the level of the floor in the house. In many cases, the garage floor is a step or two down from the house. If you like the idea of a sunken family room, fine; if not, you can build up the floor. But be sure to consider what that will do to the ceiling height. Maybe an open-to-the-rafters cathedral ceiling is the solution in this case, even if it means doing without additional storage. *(continued)*

IN THE GARAGE

(continued)

Once you've insulated your new garage room with the appropriate insulation and stapled up a polyethylene vapor barrier, it's time to turn your attention to the floor. Even though your garage's concrete floor may be high and dry and perfectly smooth, it's still a good idea to put down a subfloor before finishing the space off with tile, wood, or carpet. Why suffer with cold feet in a brand new room?

To guard against condensation, sweep the floor clean and apply a coat of concrete sealer. After it dries, snap chalk lines on the floor at 16-inch intervals. Next, run a ribbon of construction adhesive or wood-to-concrete mastic along each line. Press 1x3 "sleepers" into the mastic and level them with shims where needed. Use concrete nails, placed about 24 inches apart, to attach the sleepers to the concrete. Fit rigid foam insulation between each of the sleepers. You don't have to glue the insulation down, but to eliminate the possibility of squeaks later, it's a good idea. Finally, staple a vapor barrier of 4-mil polyethylene sheeting over the sleepers and the insulation to prevent dampness.

Once you've created a moisture- and cold-resistant foundation, the next step is to nail down sheets of ⅝-inch particleboard or Grade C-D plywood (the C side should face up). Finally, add a layer of ¼-inch hardboard underlayment (rough side up), installed perpendicular to the plywood.

Now you have a firm footing for the finish flooring of your choice—ceramic or vinyl tile, tongue-and-groove wood strips, parquet, or carpet. Make the installation of the

Nailing into concrete is hard work. To make the job easier, use a concrete nail set and special fasteners designed to work with it. The naillike fastener is held inside the nail set, a device with a large head that, when struck, drives the nail through the wood and into the concrete. With 1x3 sleepers use 2½-inch concrete nails or fasteners.

To assure yourself a room that is warm and dry, use a heavy-duty staple tacker to make quick work of installing a polyethylene vapor barrier over the subfloor sleepers and the rigid foam insulation. For walls, apply the plastic sheeting over batt or blanket insulation that does not have a built-in vapor barrier.

For a strong subfloor, nail ⅝-inch particleboard or plywood over the 1x3 sleepers. Stagger the 4x8-foot sheets so the joints occur randomly and do not end up on the same sleeper all the way across the room. Top the Grade C-D plywood with a layer of ¼-inch hardboard underlayment, nailed rough side up and perpendicular to the plywood.

Whether the board paneling you choose has a tongue-and-groove system or simply butts together, it's vital that the first board you nail to the studs (starting at the floor) is perfectly level. If the paneling is designed to overlap like siding, level each board individually before you nail it in place.

final flooring material one of your last jobs. That way you won't have to worry about damaging or soiling it while putting up drywall or paneling.

Paneling garage walls
With the ceiling and the subfloor out of the way, you're clear to start work on the walls. Drywall is the most frequently used wall surfacing material, but prefinished paneling, available in 4x8-foot sheets or in single boards, eliminates the need to patch, sand, and paint.

If you install board paneling vertically, put 2x4 cross members between the wall studs about a third of the way up from the floor and a third of the way down from the ceiling. Otherwise, you'll have only the top and bottom plates to nail the paneling to.

If you're going to put up the paneling horizontally, cut the boards to various lengths and stagger the arrangement so that the end joints don't line up in one floor-to-ceiling row. Start at the floor and level the first board so each additional board will be level as you move up the wall. If there's a gap at the floor, you can conceal it with baseboard molding. Some paneling boards are designed to overlap each other like exterior siding, in which case you'll need to level every piece as you go.

If you opt for prefinished 4x8-foot sheets of plywood or hardboard paneling, it's a good idea to put up drywall first, then glue and nail the paneling to it. Sheet paneling is not intended to bridge long or wide gaps and, without a sound drywall backing, it's likely to warp.

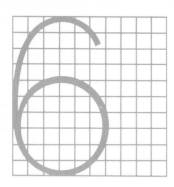

CONVERSION CASE STUDIES

Turning the raw, utilitarian spaces of garages, basements, and attics into new and livable rooms can be among the most rewarding home improvements you take on. The size, shape, and configuration of these unfinished areas may place some limits on your imagination, but if you think of a project more as an addition than a remodeling, you'll find lots of room for creativity. This chapter shows three conversions that might inspire you to look at the potential of the unfinished spaces at your house in a new way.

REMAKING A BASEMENT

The elegant pastel- and jewel-toned room shown *opposite* once was part of an earth-floored basement. It's still below-grade, of course, but the resemblance ends there. Several structural and material changes contributed to this new look.

The floor and an old concrete walkway that covered a small portion of it were resurfaced with concrete and then carpeted; several area rugs atop the carpeting help define traffic patterns through the room, as well as its use zones. A nonbearing wall in the center of the main space came out to open up the area, and an efficient and attractive wall storage system was installed along the concrete foundation wall.

To maximize the versatility of this imaginatively designed space, the homeowner chose to organize it into several zones. In addition to the family room pictured here, there's a new bath (just beyond the stairway), a new bar (to the left rear out of camera range), and a Murphy bed (also out of camera range), which provides comfortable sleeping for overnight guests. The original utility room is tucked behind the new bath and stairs and is accessible from outside.

Planning your "new" basement

Whether you opt for a large open room or a series of smaller rooms, divided by full- or partial-height walls, the time to plan the layout is before installing any new walls, ceilings, or floors or removing any original partitions. Be sure, also, to check with your local building department so your finished basement will meet all codes.

Keep in mind that because basements probably have fewer doors and windows than other levels of your home, you'll have more wall space in a finished basement than in most aboveground rooms. This makes it easier to arrange furniture and plan interesting wall treatments. Also consider building a storage wall to separate two or more areas of your basement. A storage wall adds visual interest, and the vertical lines of a floor-to-ceiling divider will visually push up a low ceiling.

If your basement is close to grade on one or more sides, you have the option of installing large windows or even patio doors. If yours is not a walkout basement, you probably will have to do without vistas and abundant natural light. Thus, the kind of lighting you install is especially important. Uplights and wall sconces provide effective overall light. Directing light upward helps to visually raise a low ceiling and minimize any down-in-the-basement atmosphere.

If your basement is dry—and it should be if you're planning to use it as additional living space—there's no reason not to carpet the floor, or even install a wood floor. Many new carpeting materials are mildew-resistant and antimicrobial, so even if your basement is a bit damp they won't be damaged. Whatever flooring material you choose, make sure it's suitable for use below-grade.

For furniture, you can use the same styles that are appropriate in upstairs rooms. Keep in mind that low-profile, scaled-down chairs and sofas tend to make any room seem larger. If you are converting your basement into a play space for children, be sure upholstery—as well as flooring materials—is durable and washable.

(continued)

REMAKING A BASEMENT
(continued)

W hen you go down the basement stairs pictured on the preceding page, the view you get is the one shown here. The window is an unusual plus for a basement, made possible because the house is on a sloping lot and the window side of the basement is partly above-grade. The door to the right of the desk leads to an outside entry. Look carefully at the wall behind the chairs and you'll see a handle up near the ceiling—that's where the Murphy bed is.

Even if you don't have a sloping backyard, you can find other ways to add daytime light to your basement. For example, consider excavating a light well around an enlarged but otherwise typical basement window. If space permits, you could even create a giant light well in the form of a sunken patio. Local building codes often require a secondary fire exit in any basement used as living space. If you don't already have direct access to the outdoors from your basement, you might want to install a new door to open onto the new patio. For more about a basement remodeling that opens to the outside and gains lots of natural light, see pages 30 and 31.

Can a basement be pretty?
Whatever your basement's natural light quotient, color can lighten and brighten a down-under space. For best results, stick to the light side of the palette: whites, neutral beiges, soothing pastels, and a few vibrant jewel tones for accent. Color the major surfaces— such as ceilings, walls, floors, and counters—with pale hues. This will create an envelope of lightness.

UPDATING AN EARLIER CONVERSION

In many older homes, the basements have gone through at least one conversion already. Although the initial remodeling may be out of date, consider yourself fortunate if you've inherited such a space: Much of the most difficult work has been done for you. To update such a basement, consider several courses of action.
• First, think about reallocating space according to function. If you have one big space, divide it according to your needs, perhaps creating a hobby room or home office along one wall or in a corner.
• Refinish old (often yellowed knotty-pine) paneling by bleaching or painting it. Because furring strips are in place behind the paneling, it's a fairly simple matter to replace the paneling with drywall, if that's the look you're after.
• Consider replacing old acoustic ceiling tiles with drywall or a suspended ceiling. If you're doing that, also think about installing updated recessed lighting fixtures to brighten the room.
• Check the floor for signs of moisture. If the old tile (often asphalt or cork) is sound, it's an easy matter to tile or carpet over it.

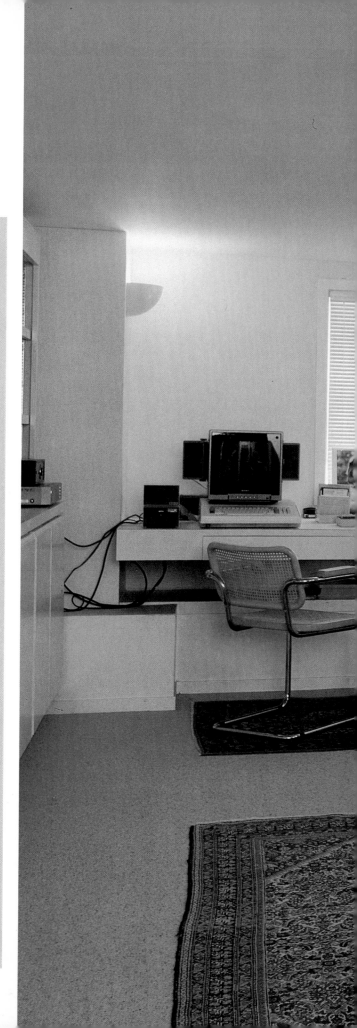

CONVERSION CASE STUDIES

When space is at a premium, devoting an entire attic to the storage of hand-me-down furniture, outgrown clothes, and seasonal accessories amounts to a painful waste of resources. Under the roof beams of most houses resides a den, family room, or bedroom just waiting to happen. The major components—roof, floor joists, and outside walls—are already in place. All you have to do is fill in the blanks and turn the shell into functional and comfortable quarters.

OPENING UP AN ATTIC

The seating area pictured *at left* has all the charm of a dream attic, and none of the closed-in dimness of many real ones. This cheerful niche is just part of a whole-attic remodeling that turned a 37x10-foot attic into a suite that seems much better proportioned than its long, narrow dimensions suggest.

The key to this transformation is a large dormer that was added to the roof's front slope. The window seat shown here follows the lines of the dormer. Besides providing seating, the arrangement offers storage, color, and a neat definition of the space-within-a-space. For more about the rest of this attic, see pages 94 and 95.

If you're planning to "do something" with your attic, you've probably already considered adding dormers. Keep in mind that dormers come in different shapes and sizes, and that their aesthetic effect ranges from minimal to major.

Often, a pair of small dormers added to the front of a story-and-a-half Colonial can lend considerable charm to the facade; a large dormer added at the back provides more space and changes the public face of the house less. Although it may seem like a safer decision to make an addition at the back, a well-designed front dormer can furnish an unexpected architectural plus.

Adding dormers may also provide a practical benefit at middle and late stages of construction: If their window openings are fairly large, you may be able to hoist building materials and even some furniture through them, an easier task than carrying bulky items through the entire house. To learn more about building dormers, see pages 116 and 117.

(continued)

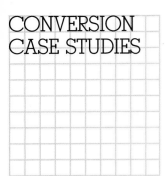

OPENING UP AN ATTIC

(continued)

A s the floor plan *below, right* shows, the dormer provides a focal point for virtually the entire attic suite, but a lot more is going on here than just a well-planned window seat with a good view.

For example, a sleep-study zone, visible toward the left in the photograph *opposite,* measures 16x10 feet and provides plenty of practical space for the homeowners' college-student daughter. Across the sitting room from the study area, and visible toward the right of the photograph, is a wall of shelves for books and records and closed storage for a host of other items. The bath/dressing area, out of camera range to the right, provides an additional wall of storage, this time for clothes.

Smooth surfaces, simple lines, and roll-out counters offer generous work space and maximize the open feeling

of this conversion. Fixed-glass wraparound windows—custom-made with mitered corners to allow for a seamless view—add a touch of drama to the sleek setting. Operable windows on the long side of the dormer look out on an appealing vista. They also provide excellent ventilation—a key consideration in any lived-in attic space.

As this conversion case study indicates, dormers don't just add light and air to an attic: They also offer partial solutions to that common attic problem, insufficient head-room. The very nature of a pitched roof means that portions of an attic won't be high enough for most adults to stand up straight in; because dormers add height along the outside walls, they bring more standing room with them. Use low-ceilinged space near the knee walls for seating or less-frequently used storage.

FIRE SAFETY IN CONVERTED SPACES

Whatever the requirements of your local building codes, any new living space in your home—whether a converted attic, basement, or garage, or a simple add-on—calls for fire-safety devices and fire-escape routes.

Perhaps the most important item is an early-warning smoke detector, preferably one that has a built-in light to illuminate nighttime escape routes, which, incidentally, should always be planned and rehearsed *before* you need them.

Particularly in attics that now function as bedrooms, a smoke detector can provide a necessary margin of safety for sleepers if a fire should break out down below. Install the detector on the highest point of the ceiling, perhaps on a hallway near the new bedroom or at the top of the stairs that lead to the attic.

Getting out
A smoke detector can't save lives, however, if there's no fast and easy way to get out in case of fire. That's why standardized building codes typically dictate stairway width—36

to 40 inches—and height—80 inches of headroom. Codes also call for attic windows to be a minimum of 24 inches long and 20 inches wide, with sills no higher than 44 inches from the floor. Most building codes also require that any room—on any level—used for sleeping must have at least one window or exterior door to permit emergency escape.

Putting the fire out
Most people keep a fire extinguisher in or near their kitchen. A better idea, however, is to keep one within easy reach on every floor of your home, including the attic and basement—even if you haven't put those areas to everyday living use. Widely available at department stores, home improvement stores, and hardware stores, the multipurpose ABC ammonium phosphate extinguisher is recommended for home use because it works on all categories of household fires: Class A (wood, cloth, many plastics, and other combustibles); Class B (gases, grease, and flammable liquids); and Class C (electrical).

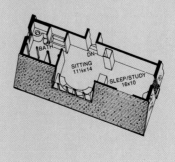

ANNEXING
A GARAGE

One reason garage conversions are so popular is they deliver a lot of living space for little money. A typical two-car garage, for example, measures about 18 by 22 feet. That's big enough for a family room, living room, or even two bedrooms. And because most garages are built with the same techniques used in house building, a garage can almost be thought of as an unfinished house. The basics are already there; what remains for you to add are imagination and the hard work that will turn all or part of your garage into full-time living space.

The highly polished wood floors, clean white walls, and quilt-hung end wall of the room and hallway pictured *opposite* don't look much like the classic image of a garage. Absent are the oil-spotted concrete floor and cobwebbed windows just above eye level.

Nevertheless, this space used to be a garage. Originally, it was appended at the back of the house behind a back porch/den, which had itself been added at an intermediate stage of the home's architectural development (see the floor plan on page 98).

Turning this afterthought garage into a welcome and welcoming new living room was a fairly simple matter for the homeowners: They replaced the double garage doors with a wall, and punctuated that wall with a series of elevated wood-framed windows that provide ample light without sacrificing privacy.

To preserve the home's country character, new oak flooring—stained to match

floors in the rest of the house—was installed, and the rafters in the new living room were left exposed, then painted. As the view *above* shows, the new exterior wall was covered with painted cedar shakes that blend perfectly with those on the main structure. The new windows, dramatic as they are, also fit in with the home's architectural features, adding visual interest without disrupting the traditional warmth that characterizes the original building.

Extra benefits
In the process of transforming the garage, the once-dark back den became an open, inviting entryway, linking the main part of the house with the former garage. You can see part of the new entry in the foreground of the photograph *opposite*. Inside the new entry now is a coat closet, deliber-

ately kept open for easy access by the young children in the family.

A new glass door and elongated sidelight window, visible from the outside in the photograph *above,* open onto a secluded brick deck angled to fit the outlines of the house. The change in the back door also allowed the owners to eliminate the door that had opened into the adjacent kitchen. As a result, they had extra room to extend the kitchen counters and reposition major appliances.

The changes at the back of the house had an important effect on the front part of the house, too, although it remained structurally unchanged. Relocating the living room to revamped quarters in back allowed the owners to turn the slightly smaller original living room into a full-fledged family room, simply by declaring that it was now a suitable place for children, pets, toys, and television watching.

(continued)

ANNEXING A GARAGE

(continued)

This garage-to-living-room story has even more to it than you might think at first and second glance. Like many garages, the one featured here had a high peaked ceiling, making space above the rafters usable. The homeowners installed flooring over about half of the rafters, creating a hideaway guest loft at one end of the room and a cathedral ceiling at the other.

The loft sleeps two, with room remaining for a small chest of drawers and a chair. A simple, open, pipe-railed stairway along the wall where the garage doors were leads to the loft.

Twin triangular clerestory windows installed at the open end of the room and visible in the photograph *below* emphasize the space's upright feeling and funnel abundant natural light straight to the main seating area. Skylights installed over the loft section, partially visible in the picture *opposite,* provide even more light. Because they're operable, they also increase ventilation. Sliding glass patio doors open to a new backyard deck, adding to the light, airy quality of the room. Additionally, the doors provide an attractive alternative route for indoor-outdoor traffic.

A freestanding fireplace with a towering chimney helps warm the room and adds visual drama. The owners also extended the home's hot-water heating by installing new baseboard units.

CAR SHELTER OPTIONS

Although turning your garage into additional living quarters for your family may well be the answer to one space problem, it does present another: What do you do with the family cars once you've annexed their home to your own?

You can, of course, build another garage if you have enough room on your lot. But building a new structure is neither instant nor inexpensive. If you have an older car that's already weathered its share of rain, sleet, snow, and sun, then perhaps a season or two outside won't do much damage. If so, you might choose to convert the garage to living space this year and build a new one next year. (See pages 100-109 for more about building a garage.)

If you don't want to leave your car unprotected, however, consider this faster and less expensive remedy:

Build a carport. Particularly in western and southern portions of the country, a carport may be all you really need to shelter your car from the elements.

With post-and-beam construction techniques, you can put up a freestanding or lean-to carport in a weekend or two. Because it doesn't require nearly as many construction materials as a garage, a carport is also considerably cheaper to build.

A compromise for northerners is to build a freestanding carport to act as a temporary shelter, then turn it into a conventional garage later by enclosing the walls and adding doors.

Still another option is to convert only half of a two-car garage to living space, leaving room for one car. This is especially practical if you want to enlarge an existing room rather than create an entirely new one.

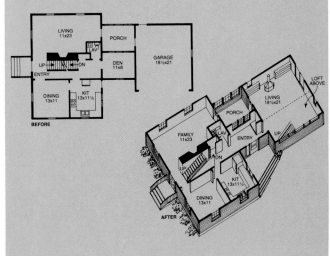

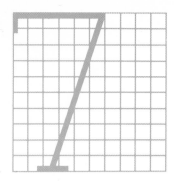

GARAGES JUST FOR CARS

If automobiles could vote, they'd unanimously want the protection of a garage. There are few better ways to protect the value of your car than keeping it out of the elements as much as possible. And square foot for square foot, garages are one of the most economical additions to any property. If you've been struggling without a garage or with a small or inadequate garage, a new one could be a good investment in your property and in the welfare of your vehicles.

PLANNING BASICS

Perhaps you've built a few closets and added lots of shelves to your house. Maybe you've even partitioned off a few rooms in an unfinished basement. But no way, you say, would you tackle a job as big as building a garage.

Yes, a garage is large, but building one isn't an overwhelming task. In fact, you may already have some of the skills necessary to construct a new home for your car.

Even if you decide to have your garage built by a general contractor or a firm that specializes in garage construction, you can help lower the cost by doing a lion's share of the planning yourself.

In many localities, you will need a building permit before you can begin a garage or any addition to your house or property. Find out what information you will need to supply to the building department before they will issue a permit. Also check whether there are any limitations about proximity to lot lines or other buildings; it may be possible to get a variance if you want to encroach on the limits. Some neighborhoods have covenants that restrict the size or site of a garage. Check for any such restrictions in your area.

Stake out a site

Now go to work looking for the best location for your garage. With stakes and string, mark out the full-size garage you plan to build. Keep these guidelines in mind: One car takes about 9x20 feet, and it's wise to build in 4-foot increments whenever possible to get the best use of sheet goods. Few single-car garages built today are smaller than 10x20 feet. Double-car garages rarely are smaller than 22x20 feet.

Pouring a garage foundation on level land is less expensive than on sloping land, but don't let the lay of the land be the determining factor. Make adjustments as necessary for the best site and then begin planning changes you'll need to make for a driveway leading to your garage.

Ask yourself lots of questions. Will you be able to back your car around? Will visitors have space to park their cars, too? If the site you've selected will require a lot of money poured into a new driveway, is there an alternative that will lower the cost for the entire project? How difficult will it be to bring electrical wires to the garage? Keep asking questions until you've found the spot.

Now consider the style of your new garage. Again, your neighborhood or municipality may have restrictions. Even if it doesn't, an addition as important as a garage should complement the style of your home, whether the garage is attached or detached. It's difficult to hide a garage, but it shouldn't call a lot of attention to itself, either. Pay attention to details: Windows, siding, roofing materials, and paint should match the house. The slope of your garage roof should echo the roof slope of the house. The garage door, because of its size, is especially important; the color or colors used here could bring undue notice to the garage.

The garage shown *opposite* was constructed from a standard plan, the same one used for the model garage you'll see taking shape later in the chapter. The two differ only in exterior materials and minor detailing. *(continued)*

PLANNING BASICS
(continued)

LAYING OUT A DRIVEWAY

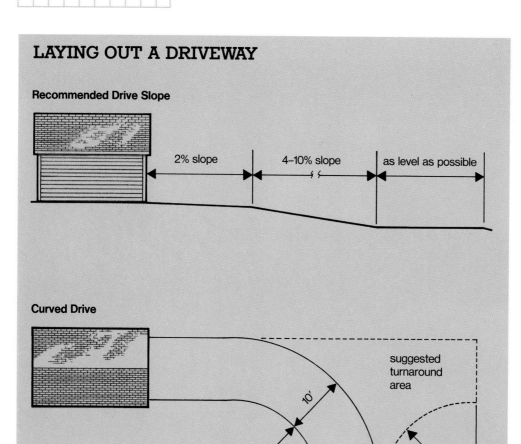

Recommended Drive Slope

2% slope | 4–10% slope | as level as possible

Curved Drive

10'

suggested turnaround area

16' radius

16' radius

As you'll see on the following six pages, framing, sheathing, and finishing off a garage are straightforward carpentry jobs that most amateur builders can master. Recruit a couple of helpers and you can probably get most of the work done in a couple of weekends.

Before carpentry can begin, however, you have to provide a firm, level slab, and at some point you'll also have to grade and pave a driveway leading to your new garage. Both are projects you might want to assign to a contractor. Not only do contractors have the skills, manpower, and equipment needed to do the work quickly and efficiently, they also know about drainage, frost lines, and other factors vital to sound, enduring surfaces.

If you don't have a lot of grading to do, have already successfully pulled off a paving job or two, and want to save money, prepare for some arduous but satisfying labor. You'll have to excavate and prepare the ground under your new slab and driveway, pour and level fill, and construct forms. Once you've laid the groundwork, call in a ready-mix truck and have enough helpers on hand to get everything poured, worked, and leveled in a single day.

The boxes *at left* and *opposite* present the basics of driveway layout and foundation work—information that is useful regardless of whether you or a contractor provides the floor and approach to your new garage.

Make a mistake in planning a driveway and you could be reminded every time a car bumper scrapes or someone gets tied up in a tight turn. The drawing *at upper right* illustrates minimum and maximum slope considerations. Adhering to these assures that cars won't bottom out and also promotes good drainage.

The drawing *at lower right* depicts the minimum radius for a curving drive. For a turnaround, plan an 18-foot length and make the turnaround at least 10 feet wide.

If heavy trucks will use your driveway, its surface material should be 6 to 8 inches thick; if only cars and light pickups will drive on it, 4 inches will be adequate. With concrete, plan for expansion joints every 15 feet.

Because of the labor and skills involved, you will probably decide to have the job done by a paving contractor. His workers will grade and prepare the site, build forms, then pour concrete or asphalt. You might engage the same firm to construct your garage's foundation. For details about this, see the box *opposite.*

POURING FOOTINGS AND A SLAB

The drawings *at right* depict two typical garage foundations—one an on-grade slab, the other a slab that rests on a frost footing. Consult local building codes to determine which will work best for your garage. The codes will also specify the minimum depth of footings and the thickness of the slab. Even if the building code does not call for reinforcing rods in the footings and reinforcing wire mesh in the slab, these are good investments.

Careful preparation of the ground under a foundation prevents cracking and settling. Remove all vegetation before preparing your base. Any roots could continue to grow and heave concrete; decaying material leaves a void that can cause settling.

If you plan to run electrical service or a floor drain through the slab, now's the time to do so. All electrical components should have waterproof seals and be specifically designed for outdoor use. If you're installing a drain, the floor should slope toward it; a floor without a drain should slope toward the door.

For the subbase you'll need 4 inches of crushed stone, sand, or both—compacted as tightly as possible. Lay a vapor barrier of polyethylene sheeting across the entire subbase, overlapping seams about 4 inches. Most building codes require an inspection before you can pour the concrete.

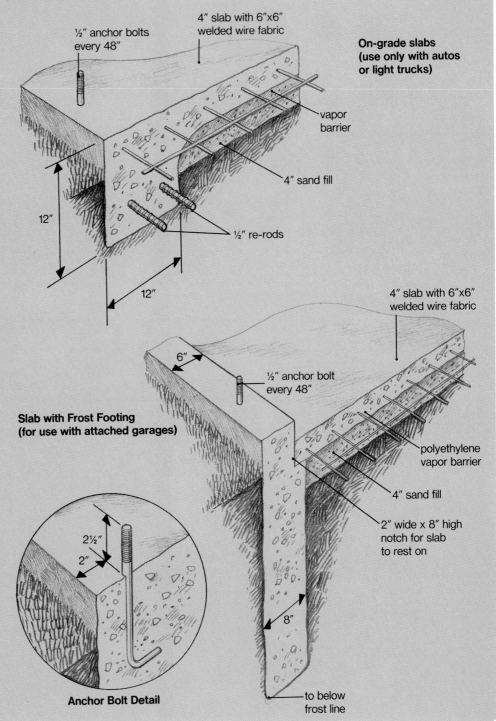

½" anchor bolts every 48"

4" slab with 6"x6" welded wire fabric

On-grade slabs (use only with autos or light trucks)

vapor barrier

4" sand fill

12"

12"

½" re-rods

4" slab with 6"x6" welded wire fabric

6"

½" anchor bolt every 48"

Slab with Frost Footing (for use with attached garages)

polyethylene vapor barrier

4" sand fill

2" wide x 8" high notch for slab to rest on

8"

to below frost line

2½"

2"

Anchor Bolt Detail

FRAMING WALLS

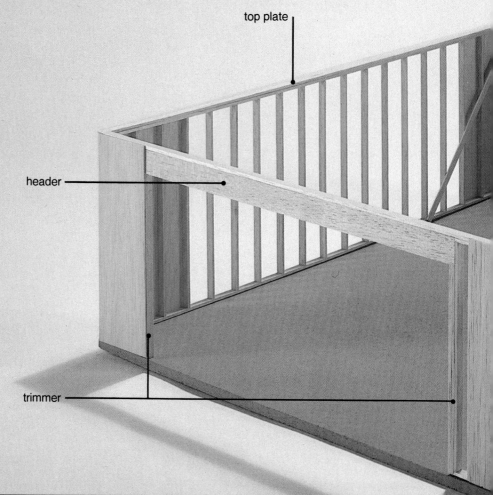

top plate

header

trimmer

Labels on the large photo *at right* identify the major elements in the framing for a garage's walls.

• *Plates*, horizontal 2x4s at the top and bottom of walls, tie together vertical members. Those at the bottom, called soleplates, are bolted to the slab; the ones up top, known as top plates, are doubled for extra strength. Select your longest and straightest lumber for plates.

• *Studs* are vertical 2x4s connecting the top and bottom plates. Our model was built with studs spaced 16 inches on center from a corner.

• *Headers* top off door and window openings. They are assembled from lumber pieces laid on edge and nailed together with ½-inch spacers between them. A header can weigh as much as 200 pounds. Installing one requires four strong people and a couple of stepladders. The next page explains how to go about this cumbersome job.

• *Trimmers* are 2x4s nailed to each side of door and window openings. They strengthen openings and help support headers.

Begin framing by laying out plates and marking out the places you will nail studs. The blades of framing squares are 1½ inches wide, the same width as the actual width of a 2x4. Align one edge of a blade with the end of a plate, then draw a line across the plate at the other edge of the blade. This marks where the first stud will go. Measure 14½ inches from this line and draw lines on each edge of the blade. Repeat the process, drawing pairs of lines 1½ inches from each other and 14½ inches from the next pair. To speed the job, lay out plates next to each other and draw lines across all of them at once.

Assembling wall sections
Drive two 16d nails through the top and soleplates into the ends of each stud, as shown *above left.* Frame any window or door openings as shown *above right.* Note that the header here consists of two 2x4s on edge with ½-inch spacers between them. Short *cripple studs* above and below further strengthen the opening.

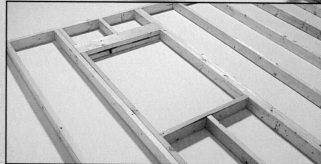

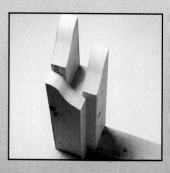

Forming outside corners
Select straight 2x4s to frame outside corners. Use three or four pieces of 2x4 blocking between two studs as shown in the photo *at right.* Later, during assembly, the stud from the second wall is nailed directly into this lumber "sandwich," as shown. This provides solid interior and exterior nailing surfaces.

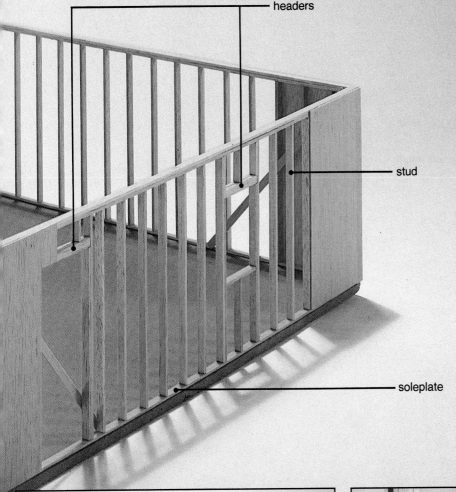

headers

stud

soleplate

Installing a garage door header

Cut trimmer studs to length and partially nail them into studs on both sides of the opening. Lift a 2x12 into place; check it for level and size. The header's top edge should be even with the top plates on both sides. Make all adjustments before driving nails home on the trimmer studs.

Assembling the header requires a second 2x12 and 11-inch-wide ½-inch plywood spacers. Sometimes, a ½-inch steel plate is added between the 2x12s for strength. Bolt the header together with ½-inch carriage bolts.

Before raising the header, rehearse the operation with your crew. Recheck for level before toenailing the header into the trimmers. After the header is secured, nail another 2x4 top plate across this span.

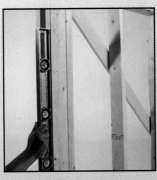

Raising walls

Before raising a sidewall, mark and drill holes in the soleplate for the sill bolts. Diagonal bracing, as shown *above,* temporarily stabilizes sidewall sections. With helpers, work together to raise one sidewall without twisting the frame. Slip large flat washers and then nuts over the sill bolts. Hand tighten; wait until walls are level and plumb before snugging with a wrench. Repeat the procedure with other walls. At corners, secure temporary diagonal braces from the top plate of one wall to the soleplate of the connecting wall. Garage construction uses additional braces not shown in this model; one end is nailed to a stud, the other to a stake driven into the ground.

Leveling and plumbing

A carpenter's level, shown *above,* is used to plumb stud walls. If the garage floor is terribly out of level, loosen braces at one corner and drive shims beneath the soleplate to adjust the level of each wall. Check the plumb (perpendicular alignment), renail the braces, and repeat the procedure at another corner.

Tightening up

When all walls are level and plumb, drive 16d nails to secure corners, then tighten nuts over soleplate bolts until the washers begin to pull into the wood. Cap the first top plate with a second top plate. For added strength, be sure to overlap layers of plates at the corners and at any other joints in the top plate.

FRAMING
THE ROOF

Today most garage roofs are framed with prefabricated trusses. Even though trusses are more expensive, they reduce the number of errors possible in measuring, marking, and cutting.

However, if you want the slope of your garage roof to match the pitch of your house roof, you may need to frame rafters the old-fashioned way. The job requires skill, patience, and accurate checking of measurements, but it's far from an impossible task.

Whichever type of construction you choose, you will have to determine the roof's slope. If, as in the garage model on these pages, you want the rise to be 4 feet, the slope is expressed as a 4-in-12 roof. This means that for every 4 inches in rise, the run or horizontal line extends 12 inches. The box *below* explains how to lay out rafter cuts.

MARKING RAFTER CUTS

If you elect to frame a roof with rafters, rather than with trusses, you first need to determine how long each rafter must be, then mark for angled *plumb cuts* at the ends and at the *bird's mouth* where the rafter rests atop a wall. Both are jobs you can do with a framing square.

You can determine the rafters' length by looking at marks embossed on the square. If, for example, you want to build a roof with a 4-in-12 slope, look on the first line of numbers beneath 4 inches on the square's front, the surface with the manufacturer's name on it. The number "12 65" tells

you that for every foot of run, the rafter will have to be 12.65 inches long. If the run is 12 feet as with this garage, the hypotenuse would be 12 feet 7¹³⁄₁₆ inches long. Deduct half the thickness of the ridgeboard and add the rafter's tail (the distance it will project beyond the wall) to determine the exact length of the rafter.

Now mark the plumb cut where the rafter and ridgeboard will join. Hold the square as shown. Use the scales on the outside of the square's *tongue* and *body* to align the slope dimensions.

To determine where to make the *heel cut* of the

bird's mouth, add half of the ridgeboard dimension before measuring the distance from the ridge. Align the 12- and 4-inch marks against the rafter as shown. The level mark for the *seat cut* is made where the body of the square meets the heel mark at a point 1½ inches from the edge.

Finally, make the rafter *tail cut,* which is parallel to the heel cut and the ridge cut. Check the fit of this rafter, then use it as a pattern for marking the others.

LAYING OUT A PLUMB CUT

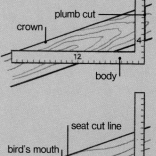

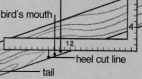

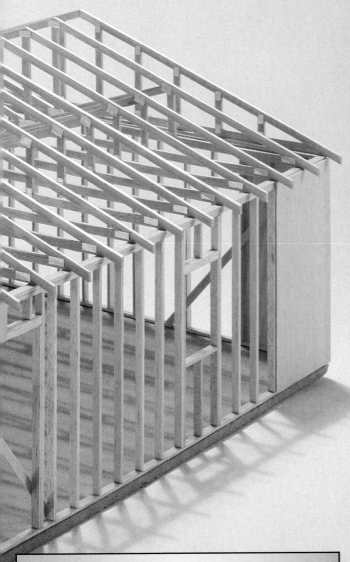

Erecting trusses

Using prefabricated trusses, like the triangular units shown *above,* you can complete an entire roof in a few hours. This type of construction eliminates the ridgeboard and instead relies on sheathing and webs of lumber for rigidity.

To order trusses, specify the span between the walls, the amount of overhang, the roof's slope, and whether you want plumb or square rafter tails. It takes at least three people to lift and swing each truss into place; have long pieces of dimensional lumber on hand to help guide and align the trusses and tie them together until sheathing is installed.

Erecting the ridgeboard and rafters

Erect a rafter at one end and temporarily nail into the top plate. On the opposite side, nail in the mate to the first rafter while a helper supports both rafters at the ridge. Temporarily nail the ridgeboard into place between the pair of rafters. A gable stud at each end temporarily supports the ridgeboard so the framework of rafters can be erected. Erect a second pair of rafters in the middle of the roof and put a third pair at the oposite end. Make adjustments as necessary to level the ridgeboard before driving the nails home. Framing anchors to make this job easier are available at home centers.

Adding rafters and finishing gables

Cut additional 2x6s to length and make the bird's mouth cuts. The rafters should be spaced either 16 or 24 inches on center; nail into the cross ties, top plates, and ridgeboards. After all of the rafters are in place, use a level to plumb the marks for the rafter tails. Finish the gable ends with 2x4s. One 2x4 should be centered directly below the ridgeboard. Cut additional studs in pairs, spacing them on 16-inch centers to the eave line. To help cool your garage, you may want to allow for a vent opening at both ends.

FINISHING THE SHELL

With the roof framed, the hardest work is out of the way. Now it's time to put up sheathing, a job that goes fast because you're working with big 4x8-foot panels.

As you may have noticed on the preceding pages, our model garage already has a pair of plywood panels at each corner. Exterior-grade ½-inch plywood here does a lot to make a garage sturdier. Be sure to leave an expansion space at the panel ends.

Plywood's superior rigidity isn't needed along the length of walls, so, for economy, we chose to cover them with ½-inch nail-base fiberboard sheathing. Because the fiberboard and plywood are the same thickness, they provide a smooth base for applying siding. Leave ⅛-inch expansion spacing between panels and at the panel ends.

Once you've sheathed the walls, turn your attention to the roof. Up here, exterior-grade ⁵⁄₁₆-inch plywood is the minimum thickness you should use with 16-inch rafter spacing; if the rafters are 24 inches apart, as they are with this roof, use a minimum of ⅜-inch-thick sheathing. Besides providing a solid base for nailing roofing materials, sheathing makes the roof stronger. A quality grade of C-D plywood is adequate for sheathing. Apply it with 6d nails spaced 6 inches apart at the edges and 12 inches elsewhere.

Next roll out and staple down roofing felt, sometimes called building felt. Start at the eave line and overlap the felt as you move up the roof. Before installing shingles, install metal drip edging around the perimeter.

Sheathing walls

If you framed your walls with studs cut to 7-foot-5⅝-inch lengths, the thickness of plates at the top and bottom of the walls will bring the total wall height to 8 feet, eliminating the need to trim plywood or fiberboard panels. To mark cuts for door or window openings, prop a panel against the wall and draw lines from inside the garage. After all walls are sheathed, you can remove the temporary diagonal bracing. If you use plywood panels for the siding, you may not need sheathing underneath. Check with your building department for code requirements.

Fitting soffits

To give your garage a finished look, enclose the soffits as shown in the photo *above*. First nail a 1x2 cleat to the siding so the soffit will be parallel to the ground. With some manufactured sidings you can buy matching soffit materials. Fit each soffit board to the opening and trim with quarter round *as shown*. To protect soffits from moisture damage, the fascia board should extend slightly below the quarter round at the eave.

Painting the garage

If there has been no rain for several days, begin applying two or more coats of paint or stain to the garage. Prime or apply the first coat of stain before filling any holes and caulking gaps. Try to match the color of the house as closely as possible. You also may want to install gutters and downspouts to direct water away from the garage; home improvement centers sell components that make this easy.

Sheathing and finishing the roof

If you followed your pattern rafter, the rafter tails should be equal in length; if not, make any adjustments now. Nail fascia boards to the rafter ends. Then start at the eave line and tack the first sheet of plywood to the end rafter.

Check the end gable for plumb before driving additional galvanized nails. Note in the photo *above* how the vertical joints of sheathing are staggered. Now apply roofing felt and drip edges to protect the sheathing from moisture damage. Finally, nail asphalt shingles on top of the felt.

Installing windows and doors

Before applying siding, fit windows and doors into their rough openings, shim them for level and plumb, then nail through their frames into the studs. Now apply siding, and caulk around window and door frames for a good seal.

CHOOSING AND INSTALLING A DOOR OPENER

Funny thing about automatic garage door openers: They're easy to live without, but once you've enjoyed the convenience of these wonders, they seem like a necessity. Day after day, openers raise and lower doors, making life easier for homeowners.

If you're considering buying a garage door opener, first determine whether your garage can accommodate one. With many openers, you must have a minimum of 3½ inches of headroom between the rafters or ceiling and the highest point the door reaches when opening. The track and power unit of most openers extend about 11 feet back from the garage door; some tracks can be shortened with factory assistance. Also be sure to measure the height and width of your door.

Next, make sure your garage door is operating correctly. It should lift and lower smoothly and not stick, jump, or bind. More about this on pages 144 and 145.

You may have to choose among two or three types of openers. An enclosed threaded rod is the heart of screw-drive units. The system shown *at upper right* is chain-driven and is lubricated with light oils. Screw-drive units are susceptible to sticking in cold climates if lubricated with grease that freezes in sub-zero weather. The newest type of opener is a less-expensive plastic-tape opener.

If you plan to install your own opener, you probably can do so in less than a day's time. Instruction manuals in do-it-yourself kits walk you through the steps.

When comparing garage door openers, consider these features and options:
• *Safety features.* The opener you install should have a safety reverse; if the door hits an object while closing or opening, it automatically reverses.
• *Manual disconnect.* If you need to open your garage door during a power failure, a manual disconnect allows you to do so (see the cord hanging below the traveler in the photo *at lower right*). If you don't have a side door or window to get into your garage to pull the manual disconnect, shop for an opener with an accessory *emergency disconnect lock* that allows you to pull a cable through a special lock and open the door from outside.
• *Transmitter codes.* The wider the range of code selections, the less chance there is that a neighbor's transmitter can open your door.
• *Keyless entry* and *electric key switch.* These are nice accessories that mount to the outside of the door and are especially handy if you don't have a side door to your garage. When it's inconvenient to get your transmitter, either punch in your private code or use your key to open the door.

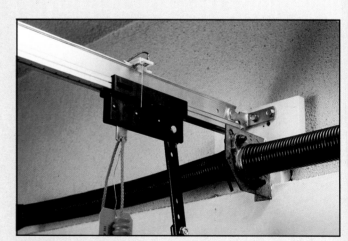

A *plastic-tape drive* can bind if improperly installed and maintained, but is replaced easily. The *traveler* moves on a metal track and pulls the garage door up as it moves toward the power unit. It is important that the *header bracket* attaching the track to the garage is tightly secured above the center of the door. The cord dangling below the traveler is the *manual disconnect* and is used during a power failure.

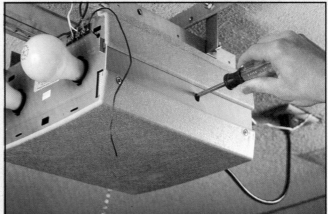

The *door bracket* should be securely attached 3 to 6 inches below the top of the door, depending upon manufacturer's instructions for your type of door. It is critical to proper operation that the center of the *header bracket, door bracket,* and *power unit* all be aligned with the center of the door.

The power unit should have easy access to adjust screws or knobs for *safety reverse* and the *open and close limits*. If young children play around your garage, you may want to increase the sensitivity of the safety reverse; check this function every month. You should be able to stop the door with both hands. The open and close limits restrict how far the door travels when raising and lowering.

WHAT ELSE CAN A GARAGE DO?

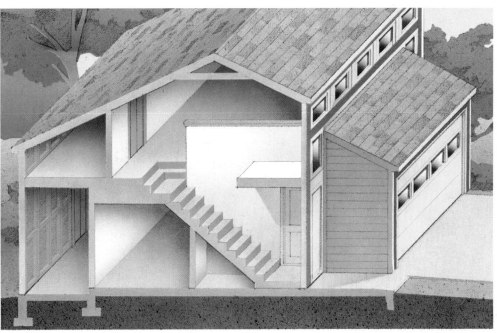

Could your home benefit from more storage, additional work space, or places to pursue hobbies? If the answer is yes, and you're thinking about building a garage, consider expanding it to take the space strain off other areas of your house.

The super-garage shown here, for example, does a lot more than just shelter a couple of cars. It also includes a potting shed, storage for lawn and garden tools, a workshop, attic storage, and an upstairs retreat for a teenage drummer.

Nestled between trees at the back of a wooded lot, this 24x36-foot structure complements the design of the house. Up top, a row of clerestory windows echoes the home's window arrangement. Siding, roofing, and other materials

are the same used on the house. The colors are identical, too, but here the scheme has been reversed.

The south-facing clerestories also soak up a lot of sun in winter months, helping to heat the low-ceilinged musician's quarters. A stairway from the drive, visible in the plan view *above,* leads to this loft and to a 24x7-foot attic storage area behind it. Look closely at the photograph *at left* and you can see a second-story deck on the right side. A sliding glass door provides access from the studio to the deck.

On the main floor, cabinets salvaged from a kitchen remodeling project were used in

the potting shed/workshop that runs the width of the garage through its center. A separate door and concrete ramp leading to this area and to the back of the garage make it easy to get equipment in and out. The same hallway, on the right side of the building, also leads to a storage area for garden gear in the rear.

Alternatives

What else a garage can do depends largely on what you need and are willing to spend. Invest in proper insulation and heating (a wood-burning stove might be all you'd need), and a garage could become an all-year workshop, auto repair bay, or art studio. In some communities, you might even be allowed to include an income-producing apartment. (To learn about zoning and code considerations that govern rental units, see page 29.)

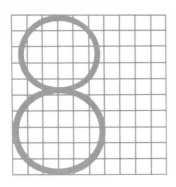

SPECIAL FEATURES

Your initial inspiration for converting a garage, basement, or attic simply may be the desire for more living space. As you begin to plan, however, let your thoughts take you beyond the essentials. Have you ever longed for a relaxing sauna, a romantic fireplace, or a sun-drenched greenhouse? Your about-to-be-converted space may be just the place to include these or other amenities. Make up a family wish list in the early stages of planning, then consider the feasibility and desirability of each item. This chapter focuses on five special features you might want to incorporate.

ADDING AMENITIES

Some "extras" add so much to a room that once you have them you wonder how you ever did without them. Others may turn out to be expensive features you seldom or never take advantage of. The key to successfully customizing your garage, basement, or attic is to keep the needs and life-style of your family firmly in mind.

If you'd like to expand attic space with a dormer, for example, will you be happy with a small one that creates a private reading nook, or do you need increased headroom throughout the space?

Some additions, such as fireplaces and wood stoves, entail a fair amount of labor, even after they're installed. You'll need to haul wood, dispose of ashes, and keep the chimney clean, for example. Nonetheless, the owners of the master bedroom pictured *opposite* find that the charm and energy savings contributed by the wood stove well outweigh the effort of feeding its fire.

Certain amenities, such as skylights, can so change a space for the better that you may find more elaborate improvement plans unnecessary. A dingy attic might appear cramped because it lacks light. Flood the same space with a bank of skylights, and you may discover you have all the space you need without building a dormer.

Similarly, planning a conversion that takes advantage of solar energy can reward you with new living quarters that cost little or nothing to heat.

When thinking about special features, think about practicality, too. It's impor-

tant, yes—but it's not everything. Even so-called "luxuries," if they contribute to your family's enjoyment of everyday life, can be practical in their own right.

Saunas fall into this category. Most of us have gotten along without them for years, but soon grow addicted to the healthy physical feeling that comes from a good sweat followed by a cool shower.

Amenity alternatives

Dormers, skylights, wood and solar heating, saunas—this chapter tells about the most popular garage, basement, and attic amenities, but your wish list needn't stop with them. Here are a couple of other possibilities.

• *Decks and patios* can extend the perimeters of any converted space, usually at a moderate cost. Because garages are on-grade, they are the most likely candidates for outdoor extensions, but consider what a sunken patio could do for your basement's outlook, or how a small, cantilevered sun deck could open up a new topside master suite.

• *Mini-kitchens* make special sense for family or entertaining areas that are on a floor level different from your main kitchen. And if you're a nighttime snacker or sipper, think of the joy of raiding a compact refrigerator near the bed or TV set. An 8-cubic-foot refrigerator may be all you need. Add to that a bar sink and perhaps a microwave oven, and a mini-kitchen can handle almost any light food preparation chore.

DORMERS

If you're looking to finish off an attic or convert a garage into two-level living quarters, a dormer can increase interior space, improve ventilation and day-lighting, and alter the exterior appearance of your home. But not all homes are suitable candidates for dormers. Before deciding to add one (or more), you have to answer several basic questions. First of all, can your home's construction accommodate a dormer, and would there be enough head-room up there? Second, how would a shed or gable dormer affect your home's exterior appearance? And, assuming you get positive answers to these questions, can you do all or part of the construction work yourself?

HOW TO BUILD A DORMER

Once you've opened up your roof, you'll want to frame and close in a dormer's exterior shell as rapidly as possible. Here are the tasks you must do before your home will be secure against the elements.
• *Plotting the opening.* Start laying out a dormer from the attic by driving nails through the roof to mark the corners of the planned opening. Position the opening so each sidewall of the dormer will rest directly on a rafter.

Now climb up on the roof and snap two sets of chalk lines for cutting. One set is for the shingles aligned with the *outside* edges of the old rafters that will be on each side of the dormer; the other set is for the roof sheathing aligned with the *inside* edges of the new doubled rafters you'll add to strengthen the opening. Be sure the bottom cut line falls directly above the outside edge of the top plate of the wall supporting the rafter ends.

• *Cutting.* Cut or pry the shingles away, then cut through the sheathing with a circular saw. Inside the house, erect temporary braces to support the roof while you're working, as shown in the photo *opposite, upper left.*
• *Framing.* Nail new rafters to the ones along the borders of the opening. Extend them from the ridge board to at least the bottom cut line. Now you're ready to remove the sheathing and cut out the intermediate rafters. Frame a shed dormer as shown in the illustration and in the photo *opposite, lower left.*

Gable dormers are trickier to frame because you need to carefully compute angle cuts for the rafters in its pitched roof. To learn about cutting rafters and framing a pitched roof, see pages 106 and 107.
• *Finishing.* Now you're ready to close in the dormer. Nail roof sheathing to the rafters, add metal drip edges to the perimeter, and staple building felt to the sheathing. Apply the roofing material, set the windows, flash the joints between the roof and the dormer, and apply siding material. For more about these jobs, see pages 108 and 109.

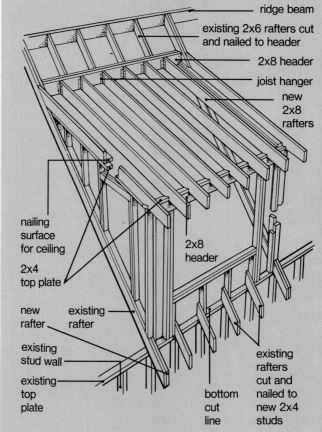

ridge beam

existing 2x6 rafters cut and nailed to header

2x8 header

joist hanger

new 2x8 rafters

nailing surface for ceiling

2x4 top plate

new rafter

existing rafter

existing stud wall

existing top plate

2x8 header

bottom cut line

existing rafters cut and nailed to new 2x4 studs

The beginning step in analyzing whether your home could benefit from a dormer is to climb up to the attic with a flashlight and tape measure and take a look around. First determine how the roof is framed. If it has trusses, rather than conventional rafters, you'll have to abandon the idea right away. (If you're unclear about the distinction between trusses and rafters, see pages 106 and 107.)

If your home has a rafter roof, get out the tape measure and measure the height from the attic floor to the ridge board up top. If this dimension is no less than 10½ feet, you can probably construct a dormer whose ceiling is at least 7½ feet high, the minimum required by most codes.

Now consider what a dormer would look like from the outside. The walk-out shed dormer pictured *below,* for example, nicely complements the appearance of a four-square bungalow; a similar dormer could make another home seem top-heavy or otherwise clash with its overall styling. In surveying your house, don't just consider the front. Often a dormer that might look ungainly from the front would blend in just fine at one side or in back.

Finally, make a realistic assessment of your carpentry skills. Not only does constructing a dormer call for advanced techniques, but the initial stages have to be completed in a day or two. For a preview of what's involved, consult the box *at left.*

SKYLIGHTS

Daylight charges a room with vitality and excitement. Skylights let in abundant light—five times as much as a side-wall window the same size—without sacrificing privacy. The dramatic 4x28-foot ridge skylight pictured *at right,* for example, brightens a newly converted attic. Light from the skylight enters an attic office/sewing room directly. A once-dark bedroom receives indirect light through a cut glass transom that is over the connecting door.

W hen choosing a sky-light for your home, consider these points:

• *Location.* If you want to gain even lighting, put your skylight on the north side of the house. But if you want to gain heat as well as light, install a skylight on the south side of the roof. Avoid placing one on a flat or nearly flat roof. If you're concerned with energy efficiency, you'll want to mount the skylight at an angle that gives the most solar gain in winter and the least in summer. Your local power company or the U.S. Department of Energy can tell you the sun's angles in your area. Instead of simply letting the slope of your roof determine the angle of the skylight, you can build up curbing, if necessary, to reach the best angle.

• *Size.* Standard skylights come in multiples of either 16 or 24 inches—the standard spacing between the centers of rafters. A skylight usually should be between 5 and 10 percent of the total square footage of the area to be lighted. The exact percentage depends on the colors of the interior space and how many windows it has.

• *Types.* The strength of a skylight can be important, especially in regions with heavy snowfalls. The three basic shapes, pictured *at left,* are the *pyramid* (the strongest shape), the *dome* (medium strength and the most popular), and the *flat* (the weakest).

• *Tints.* Panes can be clear, translucent white, bronze, or gray. Room colors appear most natural with a clear or gray skylight. Translucent white panes give a bluish-white cast to colors. Bronze panes warm up a setting. Any tint reduces the amount of light and heat passing through the pane.

• *Glazing.* Glass, acrylic plastics (such as Plexiglas and Lucite), and polycarbonates (such as Lexan and Tuffak) are used most often. Glass works well for flat skylights; select acrylics or polycarbonates for shaped skylights.

• *Fixed or operable?* A skylight that can be opened, such as the one shown *below,* will help cool your house in summer by venting rising hot air.

Compared to framing a dormer, installing a skylight is an only moderately tricky job. Most skylights come in kit form with instructions.

FIREPLACES AND WOOD STOVES

Dancing flames and crackling wood have been warming people through the ages, and the allure of a warm fire on a cold night still appeals to most of us. If you're thinking of including a fireplace or wood-burning stove in a garage, basement, or attic conversion, you first need to decide whether you'll use the new unit as a primary source of heat or only as a mood setter. Once you know what you want out of a wood-burning unit, you'll be well on your way to evaluating the different options.

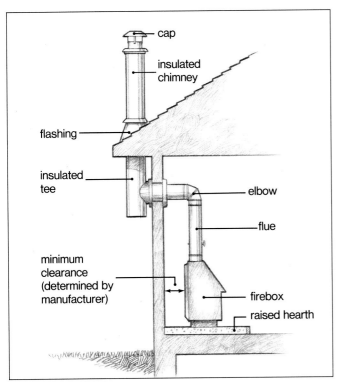

cap

insulated
chimney

flashing

insulated
tee

elbow

flue

minimum
clearance
(determined by
manufacturer)

firebox

raised hearth

An ordinary prefabricated fireplace such as the sleek unit shown *above, right* provides a delightful flame show, but don't rely on it as an energy-efficient heat source. Although you'll be warm right next to the fire, that fire will be feeding on the air in the room. If you're already heating this air by other means, the fireplace will be sending that expensive air right up the chimney.

Some freestanding fireplaces feature doors you can open to see the fire, but close when you want to boost efficiency. For other types of wood-burning units that contribute more than atmosphere, consider either a heat-circulating fireplace or an airtight stove.

• A heat-circulating fireplace is an efficient house warmer; depending on climate and the size of the room it's in, it can be a source of either primary or auxiliary heat. A heat-circulating fireplace relies on double-wall construction. Vents pull in room air and wrap it around an inner firebox. As the air heats up, it then moves back into the room in natural convection currents. Heat-proof glass doors help regulate the draft and, at the same time, let you enjoy the flames.

A version called a *fresh-air feed fireplace* employs the same basic principles, but, instead of using room air, it pulls in air from outside. In some models of either type, a small fan or blower further increases heat output.

Some heat-circulating fireplaces are freestanding; others, called "zero-clearance" models, can be built in and look for all the world like conventional masonry fireplaces.

• *Airtight stoves,* such as the one pictured *opposite,* let you regulate the draft and fine-tune a fire to peak efficiency. Air enters through an adjustable intake, then, with the help of a baffle arrangement, flows through the logs in an S-pattern that retains heat within the stove.

• *Heat-circulating stoves,* like their counterpart fireplaces, use double-wall construction to warm air by convection. These stoves increase energy efficiency, but have a furnacelike appearance.

With all airtight stoves you have to keep the door shut, so you can't view the fire.

Installation
To install a fireplace or wood stove you need to get a chimney through an outside wall or the roof. The illustration *above, left* diagrams an installation that penetrates both. Here the flue bends with an elbow to go through an outside wall, feeds into a tee, then climbs up through an eave. With prefab components like these, you can assemble a custom chimney that suits your special needs.

Besides a chimney, you also need to provide a raised, noncombustible hearth and place the fireplace or stove at safe distances from combustible and noncombustible surfaces. These are spelled out by local building codes and the manufacturer's data that comes with the unit.

If you will be ducting into an existing masonry chimney, have a professional check it out for safety before you begin your work.

SOLAR SYSTEMS

An area newly converted to living space needn't add a great deal to your utility bills. In fact, if you use solar energy for all or part of the area's heating needs, you may even be able to gather energy over and above the needs of the new space and direct the excess into the rest of the house. Solar energy systems fall into two broad categories—passive and active. A passive system uses the structure of the building to collect, store, and distribute the sun's heat. An active system uses mechanical devices for heat distribution. The best system for your conversion will depend on the size of your house, the direction it faces, the amount of sun your site receives, and the amount you can afford to spend.

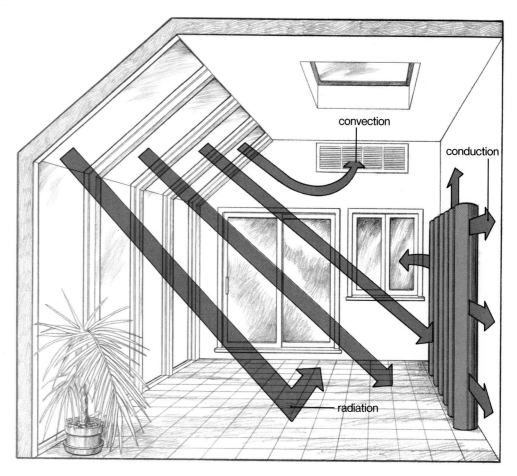

To solarize a space you must devise a way to collect the sun's heat, a method to store the gathered heat, and a means to distribute the heat throughout the space and sometimes beyond into other parts of the house.

The most popular method of *collecting* the sun's rays is to install glazing in a south wall, as was done in the sunspace pictured *opposite.* To be effective collectors, windows must face within 30 degrees east or west of true south. Glazing can be glass, which is usually the least expensive option, or clear acrylics, clear polycarbonates, or polyester reinforced with

fiberglass. To learn about other ways to collect sunlight, see the box *opposite.*

In the breezeway diagrammed *above,* the owners installed double-glazing in the south-facing wall and in the roof to maximize their solar gain. (See pages 34 and 35 for more details about this solar-efficient space.)

Thermal mass is the material that stores the heat you've let into your space. Some common heat-absorbing materials include concrete, quarry tile, brick, and water.

The most effective (and most costly) thermal mass option is to use phase-change materials. These mixtures of

chemical salts are available in a variety of containers, from small flexible plastic pouches to 6-foot-tall columns. They store and release heat by changing back and forth from a solid to a liquid state.

You can *distribute* stored heat naturally or by installing a fan. Heat travels naturally in three different ways: convection, conduction, and radiation. *Convection* is a technical term for the fact that warm air rises. If you provide a clear path for the airflow (such as the windows, doors, and vents in the drawing *above*), the heated air in a sunspace will rise and flow into the rooms behind the

space. When the air cools, it will drop and return to the sunspace, to be heated again. This convective loop will continue until evening, when the space stops gaining heat.

Conduction occurs when the sun strikes the outer face of a wall and the molecules on the surface heat up and pass along their warmth to the molecules behind them. In this way, heat stored in the back wall of a sunspace transfers to the room behind it.

When you hold your hand up to a fire and feel the heat, what you're experiencing is *radiation.* Thermal mass gives off its stored heat at night by radiation.

OTHER SOLAR COLLECTORS

If a wall of south-facing glazing doesn't suit your plans, consider the following ways to collect solar energy. The first two systems heat living space; the last two provide hot water.

• *Thermosiphoning air panels (TAP)* are shallow units installed on south-facing walls. Sun shines through a glazed pane onto an absorber plate. As the panel heats up, warm air rises through a vent at the top into the adjacent living space. Cooler household air enters the collector through a lower vent to continue the cycle.

• *Active air systems* use roof-mounted collectors. Fans pull air from the living space up into the collectors, then duct it back down. Options with air systems let you duct excess heat to rock-bin storage or to an air-to-water heat exchanger that warms household water.

• *Hot water systems* use roof-mounted collectors to warm water. In some systems the water heated by the sun is the water used in the home. In others, the solar-heated water flows into a separate storage tank where a heat exchanger captures its warmth for the household water.

• *Closed loop systems* circulate a fluid that's a mix of water and glycol antifreeze. The liquid is heated by the sun, then pumped through a heat exchanger to warm household water.

SAUNAS

If your family is fitness oriented, you may already have planned to incorporate an exercise center in a basement or garage. For after-workout relaxing, consider adding a sauna. The sauna ritual of dry-heat bathing begins with exposure to intense heat in an insulated wooden room, followed by a cool shower and a rest period. The sauna is simply furnished with two or three tiers of wood benches. A special stove, designed to hold heat-retaining igneous rocks, maintains the air temperature at 160 to 200 degrees Fahrenheit. If you have a space at least 3x4 feet, preferably near a bathroom, you have the potential for installing an at-home sauna.

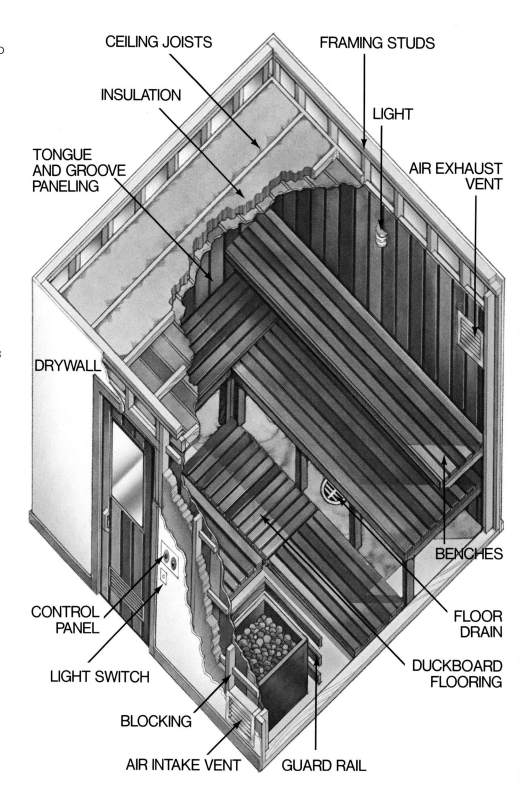

CEILING JOISTS

INSULATION

FRAMING STUDS

LIGHT

AIR EXHAUST VENT

TONGUE AND GROOVE PANELING

DRYWALL

BENCHES

FLOOR DRAIN

CONTROL PANEL

DUCKBOARD FLOORING

LIGHT SWITCH

BLOCKING

AIR INTAKE VENT

GUARD RAIL

A do-it-yourselfer familiar with ordinary stud wall construction can build a sauna in a couple of weekends. If you're less ambitious—or skilled—and willing to spend more money, you can purchase a prefabricated kit that goes together in a few hours.

To build a sauna from scratch, select only top-quality lumber, preferably cedar or redwood, which can withstand rapid changes in temperature and humidity. Look for unblemished, high-grade, vertical-grain lumber that has been kiln-dried to resist shrinking, cupping, and warping.

Panels of 1x6 V-grooved tongue-and-groove lumber work best but are expensive. To save money, the owners of the sauna pictured *at right* tongue-and-grooved boards themselves. The interior surface of the wood should be unfinished; stains or paint can emit toxic gases under high heat.

As illustrated *opposite*, walls and rafters are usually standard 2x4 frame construction on 16- or 24-inch centers, with 2x4 or 2x2 blocking pieces staggered every 2 feet horizontally between the studs.

The existing floor of your garage or basement can serve as the sauna foundation. If the floor isn't concrete, you'll need to install a 2x4 wood frame and a plywood subfloor over the existing floor. Put down a vapor barrier and use pressure-treated lumber for an easy-to-clean sauna with a floor drain.

If possible, using existing walls usually will simplify construction of the sauna room. Leave ventilation between the sauna ceiling and the ceiling of the existing structure, and between the sauna walls and any masonry walls. Insulate the walls with 3½ inches of fiberglass or its equivalent; use 5½ inches in the ceiling.

To minimize heat loss, the sauna door must have proper insulation and fit the jamb or frame. A door made of a double thickness of 1-inch redwood provides adequate insulation. For safety, the door should always open outward, and it should never have locks. Use wooden door handles and fit the door with a friction or roller catch so a bather can't be entrapped.

Wiring a sauna takes a fair amount of expertise, so you may want to have an electrician do it. Inside the sauna, you'll need a soft interior light; outside, a control panel with thermostat, an on/off switch, a signal light, and a timer.

Sizing a sauna

Start by considering how many people will be using the sauna at the same time. Six square feet per bather is ample; 3.5 square feet is the absolute minimum. If possible, plan one wall to be at least 6 feet long so a bather can lie down. The diagrams *at lower right* show typical sauna layouts.

Arranging benches in tiers makes the most of interior space. Rectangular or L-shape saunas provide the most usable space per square foot.

Selecting a stove

You can choose from gas, electric, or wood stoves. Electric stoves are most popular in the United States because they are clean, efficient, easy to install, and economical. You may prefer a gas stove, however, if it's going to cost you several hundred dollars to run 220-volt wiring to the sauna. A wood-heated sauna requires that you be near a good supply of the right kind of dense wood to burn.

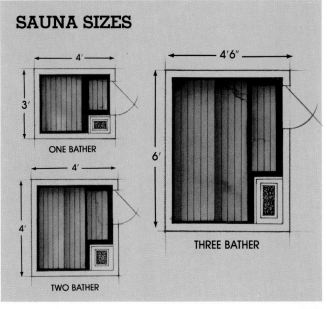

SAUNA SIZES

ONE BATHER — 4' × 3'

TWO BATHER — 4' × 4'

THREE BATHER — 4'6" × 6'

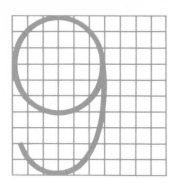

EXTENDING SERVICES

Converted spaces—intelligently designed, decorated to your liking, and made comfortable—can make your home a lot more livable. Of these three attributes, comfort may be the least glamorous, but is just as important in the long run. More than that, you want comfort at a reasonable cost. Extending existing heating, plumbing, and electrical services represents the least expensive way to make converted space as convenient and pleasant as your present living areas. In this chapter, you'll learn when you can extend services easily, and when you may be wiser to start anew.

HEATING AND COOLING

Part of a porch was taken over to enlarge the kitchen shown *opposite*. Heating this converted space was no problem: The owners simply relocated a radiator. For cooling, they decided to invest in central air conditioning, delivered through exposed ducting suspended from a random-width, wood-plank ceiling. By painting the cooling ducts to match cabinet and counter surfaces, the owners turned a potential eyesore into a decorative plus, and saved money by not furring down around the ducts. Registers cut into the ducts release air to both ends of the kitchen at ceiling level.

What's the most efficient, economical way to heat or cool a garage, basement, or attic? The answer depends in part on which space you're thinking about finishing.

Basements usually cost the least because in most cases, furnaces and central air conditioning equipment are already there. All you need do is tap existing ducts or piping.

Attics rank a close second. Since World War II, hundreds of thousands of Cape Cod-style houses built with unfinished attics usually have included sealed-off piping or duct runs to the attic. If yours isn't one of these attics, you can satisfy heating or cooling needs in one of two ways:
• Spend the money to extend systems that now reach only to the floor below, or install space heating and cooling.
• If you're hardy, you need to do very little. During cold months, simply allow heat from the floor below to rise into the completed attic space. In summer use a low-cost window fan to keep air moving and provide moderate comfort.

Extending heating or cooling to a converted garage usually costs the most. That's because most garages do not have piping or duct runs in place or even nearby.

One way to lessen the cost of bringing heating or cooling to a converted attached garage is to open it up to adjacent existing space, such as a kitchen. The heated or cooled air in the kitchen would spread naturally to the new areas. Low-cost space heating could take up the slack in winter. In summer, an air conditioner could help cool the room.

Bundle up
The box on page 131 explains how to evaluate the factors used in determining British thermal unit requirements for heating and cooling systems. One of the most important of these factors is the amount of insulation a converted space has: The fewer Btus an area loses, the fewer you need to supply to it.

Here again, most basements score well. All or at least some of your basement walls are probably underground, and the surrounding earth is a good natural insulator. Walls exposed to outside air, and all basement walls in cold climates, should have the maximum R-value insulation for your area (see pages 76-79). In a basement, however, you needn't insulate the ceiling.

In an attic you may already have some or even adequate insulation already, though you might have to add to this. To learn about insulating attics, see pages 80-83. Garages usually need the largest investment in new insulation. Pages 84-87 show how it's installed.

At openings, install double- or triple-glazed windows and insulated doors. Also, caulk and weather-strip wherever there's the slightest chance of an air leak. *(continued)*

HEATING AND COOLING
(continued)

If your present heating/cooling system has enough reserve to handle the newly finished space, by all means use it. To extend an air system you need invest only in new ducting; new piping will stretch a water or steam system; electric resistance or radiant heating would require a new circuit or two.

If the calculations presented on page 131 indicate that your present heating/cooling units could not handle the increased load, you have two options: Replace the existing system with one that has greater capacity or select a secondary heating-cooling source sized to suit the new space.

Upgrading your entire system makes sense if it's aging and would need replacing in a few years. You may discover that a new high-efficiency furnace or central air conditioner could handle both the existing house and a newly finished living space without increasing your energy bills.

Secondary heating and cooling units offer high efficiencies, too, and come in packages small and flexible enough to tuck in almost anywhere. Among the options:

• A horizontal warm-air furnace—like an upright furnace turned on its side—can fit into tight space between the ceiling of a converted attic or garage and the roof ridge.

• Upflow furnaces come in shapes slim enough to slip into a closet. An upflow furnace can heat several spaces via short runs of duct.

• A down-flow furnace works like an upflow furnace turned upside-down. It is ideal for ducts in a slab or crawl space.

• Wall-mounted knapsack-size boilers provide hot water instantly for baseboard radiators in an attic or garage.

(continued)

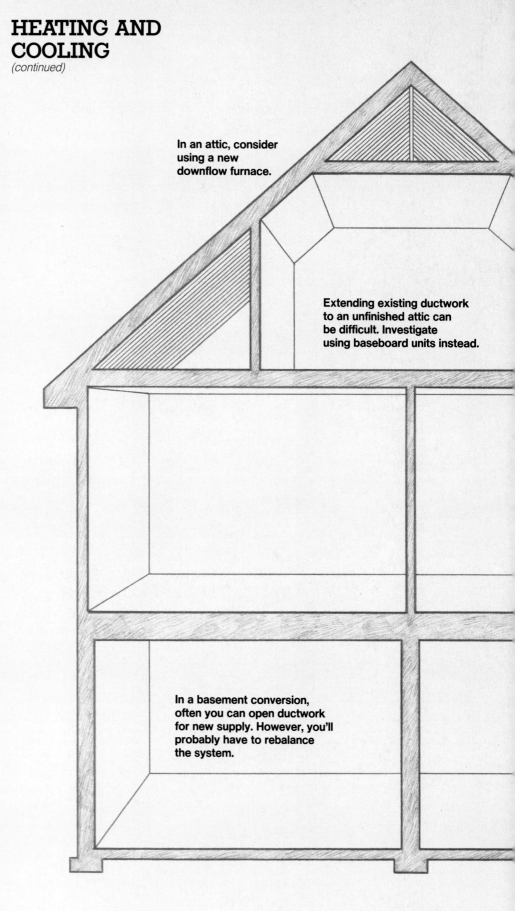

In an attic, consider using a new downflow furnace.

Extending existing ductwork to an unfinished attic can be difficult. Investigate using baseboard units instead.

In a basement conversion, often you can open ductwork for new supply. However, you'll probably have to rebalance the system.

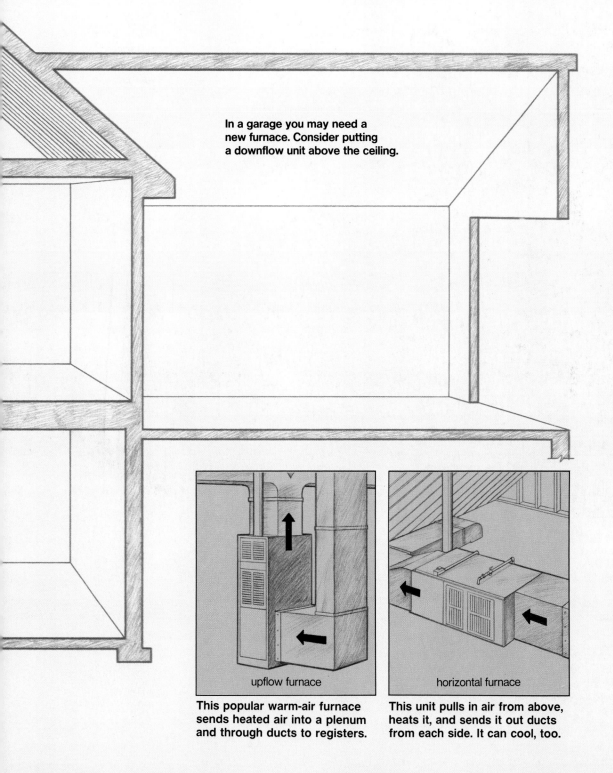

In a garage you may need a new furnace. Consider putting a downflow unit above the ceiling.

upflow furnace

This popular warm-air furnace sends heated air into a plenum and through ducts to registers.

horizontal furnace

This unit pulls in air from above, heats it, and sends it out ducts from each side. It can cool, too.

HEATING AND COOLING
(continued)

As previously noted, heating or cooling a basement planned as a family room may require no more than cutting into ducts positioned between or below the first-floor joists. This shortcut is usually possible since most furnaces and air conditioners are somewhat oversized at the start.

Installing a new register or adding a new duct run isn't hard, but you may have to tinker with the entire system afterward. When a system is installed, the contractor balances air delivery by adjusting the fan speed and manipulating dampers located in the ducts. A smooth-running system brings an even volume of air to each register in the house, even though some may be more than 25 feet apart.

Cutting open a duct changes the original air delivery balance, making it necessary to readjust the system. Try widening a damper on the run leading to the new cut and slightly closing dampers in other runs. If this doesn't bring an even flow of air to the house *and* the basement, call in a heating contractor.

You need plumbing skills to extend hot-water or steam piping. Older systems usually circulate best through pipe that has threaded connections. Newer systems employ copper piping; joints are "sweated" with a torch and solder. You'll need to drain any lines before making cuts, and rebalance the newly extended system.

To extend an electric baseboard system, your service entry must have another circuit available and the extra amperage to handle the new line. If this is the case, you need only run new wiring and install the baseboard units.

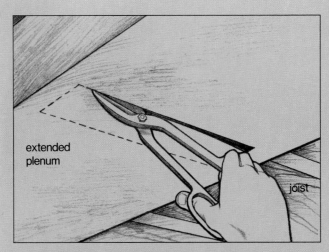

DUCTING

Cutting into an extended plenum or into one of the ducts, whichever is closest to the finished space, is a shortcut to comfort. With a marking pen, outline the cut; drill starter holes and finish with sheet-metal shears. Mount a movable-vane register in the new opening. You'll need to rebalance the system, as explained *at far left.*

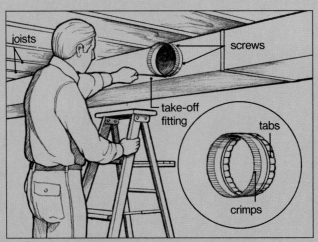

To move conditioned air to a point not now served, run a new duct there. Start by cutting a hole in the extended plenum to match a take-off fitting. Slip its tab end into the hole; bend down the tabs and screw fast with sheet-metal screws. From this fitting, extend the new duct.

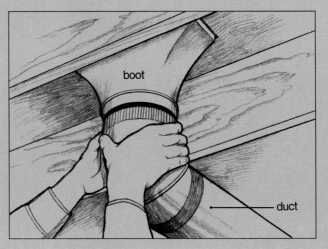

"Boot" is the name given the funnel-shaped fitting at the end of a duct. The boot connects a register—in the converted space, for example—to the duct. Since air moves more easily around curves than right angles, use elbows to soften the 90-degree turn. Once the duct and boot are in place, wrap all seams with duct tape.

WALL FURNACES

A gas-fired space heater fits between studs, as shown here, or directly over interior drywall. In some areas, building codes stipulate that a professional must install gas space heaters. And whether you or a contractor installs the unit, a gas company employee must make the gas line connection. Be sure the unit is Underwriters Laboratories (UL) approved.

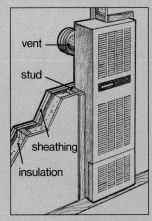

Wiring, needed to run the unit's fan, may come from below, or you might find a line in the wall to tap into. The pipe poking through the back panel supplies gas. In-wall heaters are designed to slip between studs on conventional 16-inch centers. You remove only drywall and insulation to install the heater.

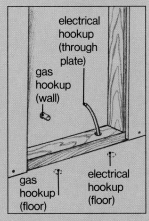

New, gas-fired space heaters don't need a conventional flue to evacuate burned gases. Nor do they draw indoor air for combustion. This compact vent combines flue and air intake. To install it, make a circular cut in the sheathing and siding to exact specifications. Place a bead of long-lasting caulk around the baffle plate's edge before pressing it to the outer wall.

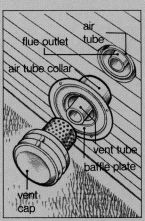

CALCULATING HEATING AND COOLING NEEDS

Although contractors calculate precise figures to determine heating and cooling needs, you can come up with a ballpark figure on your own for your converted space.

To determine heating needs, first, multiply the area's length times its width times its height to get the volume in cubic feet. Then multiply the volume by one of these factors:
- 6.5 if the house has no insulation;
- 6.0 if only the ceilings or roof is insulated;
- 5.5 for a completely insulated house;
- 5.1 if all of the house is insulated and it has storm doors and double-glazed or better windows.

Let's say you plan to turn a garage that measures 21'x24'x8' into a keeping room. 21'x24'x8'=4,032 cubic feet. You plan full insulation and double-glazed windows, so multiply the volume by 5.1. The space will need about 20,564 Btus/hour of heat. That heating need is much smaller than the lowest output furnace sold (40,000 Btus/hour), so you can rule out the feasibility of installing a second furnace. Now your options are two: Extend the present system or use space heaters.

To determine if your present system can heat the converted garage you need numbers for the rated output of the heating unit,

its age, and heating needs for the whole house. The boiler's or furnace's identification plate should list the output. Subtract ½ percent of output for each year of service. Use the formula at left to figure whole-house heating needs.

Example: Suppose rated output is 83,250 Btus/hr for a 12-year-old unit, and house-heating needs amount to 62,500 Btus/hr. Subtract 6 percent of output: 83,250 − 4,995 = 78,255. Now subtract the house needs: 78,255 − 62,500 = 15,755 Btus/hr, not quite enough for the new room.

Wall furnaces, like the one illustrated at left, come in sizes from 15,000 to 70,000 Btus/hr. One could easily heat the new space.

Rough figures for cooling needs are easy to calculate, too. Multiply length times width for area, then use these figures:
- 350-450 sq. ft. needs 9,000 Btus/hr;
- 450-520 sq. ft., 10,000 Btus/hr;
- 520-600 sq. ft., 11,000 Btus/hr;
- 600-750 sq. ft., 12,500 Btus/hr;
- 750-900 sq. ft., 15,000 Btus/hr;
- 900-1,050 sq. ft., 16,500 Btus/hr;
- 1,050-1,250 sq. ft., 19,000 Btus/hr;
- 1,250-1,600 sq. ft., 23,000 Btus/hr.

Another option is a heat pump to deliver heating and cooling to the new space.

ANATOMY OF A PLUMBING SYSTEM

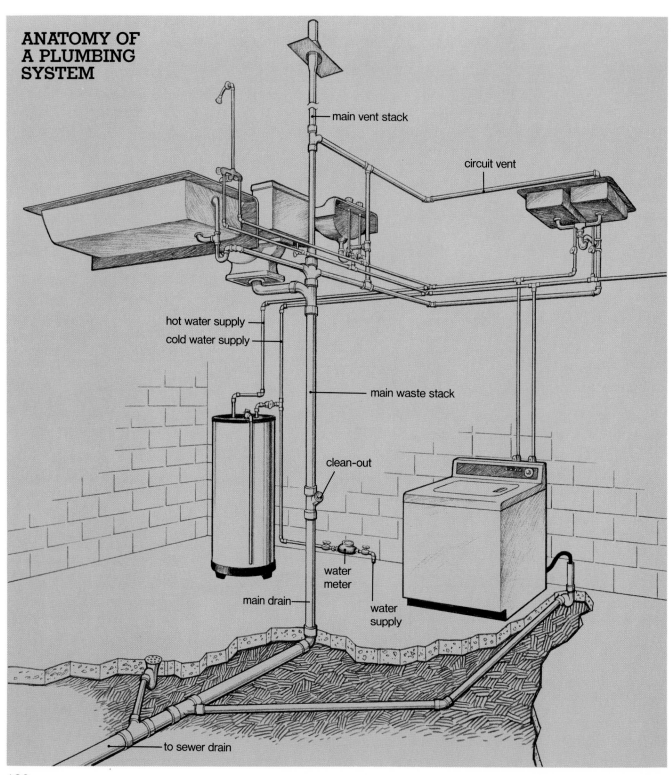

main vent stack

circuit vent

hot water supply

cold water supply

main waste stack

clean-out

water meter

water supply

main drain

to sewer drain

PIPING TYPES

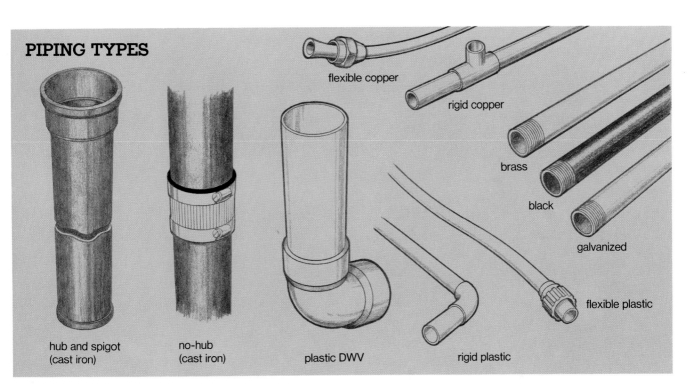

flexible copper

rigid copper

brass

black

galvanized

flexible plastic

hub and spigot
(cast iron)

no-hub
(cast iron)

plastic DWV

rigid plastic

The diagram *opposite* depicts how piping courses through your house. Small-diameter pipes deliver hot and cold water, and larger pipes remove waste water. Fresh water is pushed by pressure (about 55 pounds per square inch) from the municipal water supply or from a pressure tank in line with a private well. The force of gravity sends waste out. One or more vents in the roof help drain drains and also evacuate potentially harmful sewer gas.

If you're thinking about adding a bath in converted space, you or your plumber will need to think about how to extend existing plumbing. What you don't have to worry about is water pressure. Current pressure in the line will deliver water to the new bath, or even two new baths and a

laundry. Hot water might be a problem, however. A water heater sized for 1½ baths and used by a family of three may fall short of the needs of 2½ baths and a family grown to five.

Typically, a 30-gallon hot water tank can serve a family of four. Today, most manufacturers start residential tank sizes at 40 gallons to allow for plenty of hot water with reserve for expanding water needs.

Another consideration: If waste materials from your house go into a septic tank, additional waste from a new bath may call for more frequent tank cleanings—and there may come a time when you'll need to replace the tank

with a larger one emptying into a new field.

Planning basics

A good plan is the first step for any plumbing expansion project. Ideally, a new bath, wet bar, laundry, or powder room should be over or back-to-back with existing plumbing. This keeps piping runs short and costs down, and reduces to a minimum the mess of breaking into walls and through floors.

In all cases, select the same size piping as piping in the house now. And remember that pipe and fitting sizes are measured by the pipe's inside diameters. From a plan drawn to scale, calculate how much pipe you need. To paraphrase the carpenter's adage: Measure twice, order once.

The three piping types on the left side of the drawing *above* are for waste, or, as known in the trade, drain/waste/vent (DWV) piping. DWV components are not interchangeable with supply piping, even when they're made of the same materials. This is because drainage fittings have smooth insides. Since supply fittings are under pressure, slight restrictions barely impede the flow of water.

Pipes at the right side of the drawing are all for supply lines. To learn about selecting the right piping for your project, turn the page.

(continued)

Once you have the plan drawn for your extended plumbing system, submit it to the building department for approval. Plumbing codes apply nearly everywhere, even in most rural communities. It may turn out, for example, that you can't use plastic pipe. All national performance codes allow plastic pipe, but some local jurisdictions still prohibit its use.

The building department is more than a watchdog; it can also be a source of advice. Use it. You want your system to function properly and safely just as much as the department does.

If you intend to plumb the job yourself and are hazy on details, refer to a plumbing manual for specifics. Suppliers represent another source of help. Most large hardware stores, building materials outlets, and home centers stock the piping you want and often also rent specialized tools you may need. Usually, at least one expert is on hand to explain using the tools and assembling plumbing components. Another possibility: attend an evening class in plumbing. Vocational schools often offer such classes.

If you prefer to hire a plumber, skimming the data here will help you understand what's involved and help the two of you plan the work.

Materials options

The chart *opposite* summarizes the piping in use today. Here's a closer look:
• *Plastics* were used for piping in Europe as early as the 1930s. What you buy today has a long history of acceptable use. A coping saw cuts it. Solvent applied to the end of a pipe holds the pipe and fitting fast. You can buy special transition fittings to connect new plastic pipe with existing copper or threaded metal pipe. And as the chart shows, there are plastics for hot and cold water supply and DWV piping.
• *Copper* is currently the most commonly used metal piping. Like plastics, copper resists lime build-up in the core of the pipe, and lasts almost indefinitely. Copper joints are soldered or ''sweated,'' a job that takes some practice. Flexible copper tubing, though not meant for sharp turns, saves the use of some fittings where a wide curve is required.
• *Black* or *galvanized iron* pipe is used infrequently these days, though many older houses have it. It is inexpensive, and is often chosen for that reason. The main problem with it is that lime builds up inside at a rather rapid rate, especially in areas with hard water. Black iron or galvanized pipes are also prone to rusting, especially at fittings.
• *Cast iron*, used only for DWV piping, is heavy and hard to handle. But it has a long history of exemplary service as waste piping, and is still the standard in many areas. Hubless connections, like the ones shown *at lower far right,* simplify installation.
• *Brass* and *bronze*, much in favor early in this century, are extremely rare now.

As noted earlier, placing new plumbing fixtures near existing ones simplifies installation—because you can tap into your present DWV stack. If that's impractical, you or your plumber will have to install a new stack. The drawings *at right* illustrate the basics.

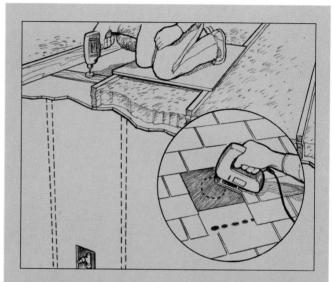

Carpentry skills are important in plumbing. Using a drill with a hole-cutter bit, bore a path for new pipes, as shown *above left.* To make a cut for a roof vent, mark the spot by pushing a nail through a hole drilled from beneath. Remove the shingle where you'll be cutting and the shingle above it. Cut with a saber saw.

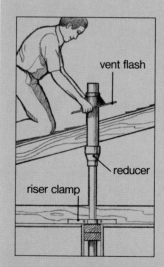

The hole's diameter should match the vent pipe's *outer* diameter. Flashing fits over the pipe, tucking beneath the shingles above and over those below the pipe. Caulk where flashing meets

the pipe and around the exposed perimeter in contact with the roof. No-hub joints for cast iron drain pipe connections have neoprene sleeves and hose clamps. Cement seals the sleeves.

CHOOSING THE RIGHT PIPE MATERIALS

MATERIAL	USES	FEATURES AND JOINING TECHNIQUES
COPPER		
Rigid	Hot and cold supply lines; DWV	The most widely used, although more costly than other types. Lightweight and highly durable. Sold in 20-foot (and sometimes shorter) lengths. Solder it together.
Flexible	Hot and cold supply lines	Comes in easily bent 60- and 100-foot coils. Solder or connect with special mechanical fittings.
THREADED		
Galvanized steel	Hot and cold water lines; DWV (not for gas)	Because it's cumbersome to work with and tends to build up lime deposits that constrict water flow, galvanized steel is seldom used anymore. Standard-length pipe must be cut, threaded, and screwed into fittings, but you can buy shorter precut sections already threaded.
Black steel	Gas and heating lines; vent piping	The main difference between this and galvanized steel is that "black pipe" rusts readily and isn't used as a carrier for household water.
Brass and bronze	Hot and cold water lines	Again, you cut and thread. Very durable but also very costly.
PLASTIC		
ABS	DWV only	Black in color. Lightweight and easy to work with, it can be cut with an ordinary saw, and cemented together with a special solvent. Some local codes forbid its use.
PVC	Cold water and DWV	Cream colored, blue-gray, or white. PVC has the same properties as ABS, but you can't interchange the two materials or their solvents.
CPVC	Hot and cold supply lines	White, gray, or cream colored. Same properties as ABS and PVC, but not interchangeable with them.
Flexible polybutylene (PB)	Hot and cold water lines	White or cream colored. Goes together with special fittings. Costly and rarely used.
Flexible polyethylene (PE)	Cold water and gas	Black. This material has the same properties as polybutylene. Used mainly for sprinkler systems.
CAST IRON		
Hub and spigot	DWV only	Joints are packed with oakum, then sealed with molten lead. Some plumbers use a special compression-type rubber gasket.
No-hub	DWV only	Joins with gaskets and clamps.

PLANNING NEW CIRCUITS

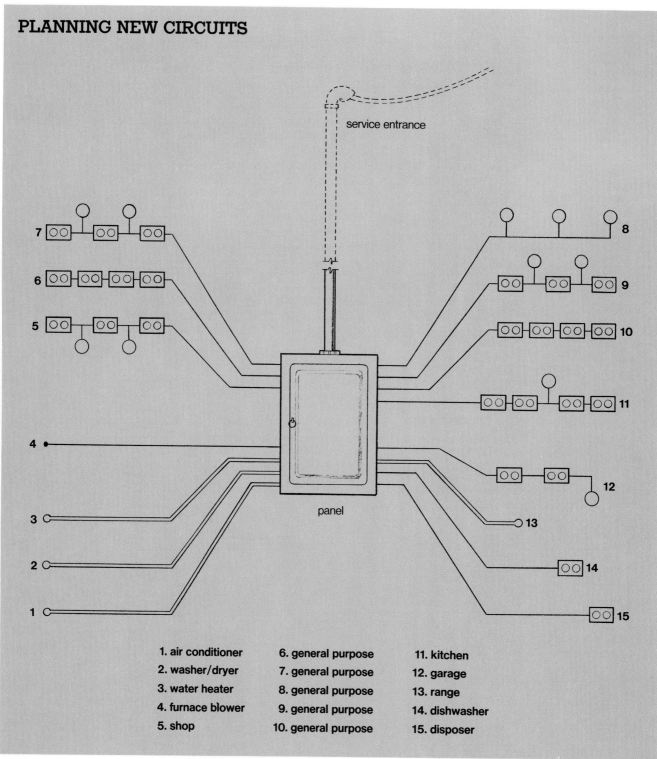

service entrance

panel

1. air conditioner
2. washer/dryer
3. water heater
4. furnace blower
5. shop

6. general purpose
7. general purpose
8. general purpose
9. general purpose
10. general purpose

11. kitchen
12. garage
13. range
14. dishwasher
15. disposer

Most garages, basements, and attics have just enough wiring to supply a light or two, and perhaps a few receptacles—far short of the circuitry needed for finished living space, and certainly not enough for air conditioning or electric baseboard heating.

Wiring frightens many people. It's true that under the right conditions, electricity can deliver a terrifying shock. This is why you always must be careful working with wiring. However, once you've turned off its power at the service entrance, wiring is as safe to handle as a cold pot or pan.

Like plumbing, wiring is governed by strict codes. Before you extend any wiring, check with local codes to determine whether your plan is acceptable and to learn as much as possible about the kind of wiring you intend to do. In fact, if you're unsure of the principles of wiring, obtain a copy of the National Electrical Code, published once every three years and updated each time. The portions of the manual dealing with residential wiring are worth a good trade school course.

In some areas, local codes forbid do-it-yourselfers to install or rework wiring at all. In others, you can wire the spaces, but cannot tie your wiring to the service entry (the fuse box or circuit breaker box that converts power from the utility to house power).

Making a plan

Regardless of whether you or an electrician does most of the work, a good wiring installation begins with a clearly drawn plan. The drawing *opposite* depicts a typical circuit diagram. Here the rectangular *panel* in the center serves as the service entrance and distributes house power to appliances, lights, and so on.

For purposes of identification, the circles on stems are fixed lighting—usually ceiling fixtures. Rectangles containing two circles are wall outlets. Single lines extending from the panel deliver 120-volt, 15-amp service, power for such things as lights, television, radio, clocks, and most small appliances. Heavy-use areas, such as the kitchen and shop, will need 120-volt, 20-amp circuits. Double lines indicate 240-volt, 20-amp power, needed for air conditioning, electric ranges, electric dryers, and some furnaces.

You can bring more power to converted spaces in one of two ways—by extending nearby existing circuits or by running entirely new circuits from the service panel. In our diagram, several circuits have only moderate loads and could be "stretched" to supply a few more lights and outlets. In all but very new homes, however, most circuits are already operating near capacity, so you'd be wiser to start afresh from the service panel.

It's also entirely possible, especially if yours is an older home that hasn't recently been rewired, that you don't even have enough power coming in at the service panel. The box *at right* explains how to assess the situation there.

Finally, check your community's code to determine what type of cable is permitted, and under which circumstances. Nonmetallic, plastic-sheathed cable is the easiest to run; metal-armored or "BX" cable is heavier and less flexible; and rigid conduit is the toughest to install. Nonmetallic and BX cable can be fished through wall and ceiling cavities, as shown on pages 138 and 139. *(continued)*

pages 138 and 139.

DO YOU HAVE ENOUGH HOUSE POWER FOR NEW CIRCUITS?

Consider the proliferation of electrical devices around most households during the past several decades and you can begin to understand why many houses have little or no power to spare for a newly converted space. Here's how you can tell if your home is at or near capacity.

Start by writing down the total amperage at the service entry. If you can't see it noted, open the panel box. In a fused system you'll find two fuses behind the main fuse pullout. Each fuse is marked with a total amperage. For example, a 200-amp service would have two 100-amp fuses in back of the pullout. In a circuit breaker panel, total amperage is marked on the tip of the main switch.

Now add up the amps used by everything electrically operated in the house. Here's how: Amps equal watts divided by volts. A 100-watt bulb on a 120-volt circuit draws 0.83 amps. Some equipment shows amperage on the identification panel.

Suppose amperage for the electrical devices in a house add up to 119.3, and the service delivers 100 amps. This house needs more power. The owner can manage for a time by not operating too many devices at one time. But a new living space would require more power—a job for the power company or a licensed electrician.

If you find yourself in this position, opt for 200-amp service, rather than stopping at 150 amps. This provides plenty of spare power and could add to the resale value of your house.

Increasing power

If you decide to bring in more amperage, consider upgrading other aspects of your home's electrical service as well. Underground wires, for example, eliminate unsightly overhead lines and reduce the chance of power outages. Or, if you have an old-fashioned fuse box, your electrician may recommend replacing it with a breaker panel. Another possibility, especially for an attic or some other location remote from the service entrance, is to run a single, high-amperage circuit from the main panel to a subpanel in the new space. From the panel you could then branch off into smaller separate circuits.

For example, let's say you want four 15-amp circuits (60 amps total) in a garage-turned-family room, and the main service panel is at the other end of the house, about 30 feet away. By running one 60-amp line from the main panel to the subpanel, you save three runs (90 feet) of the smaller gauge wire needed for the four individual circuits.

Once you've decided that you have adequate power to supply an additional circuit or circuits in a converted space, you need to install boxes for receptacle outlets, switches, and fixtures. Mounting the boxes themselves isn't difficult. You can choose versions that you nail to studs and joists (if they're exposed), or other types that attach to paneling, drywall, or plaster and lath (if the walls are already finished).

Getting wires *to* the boxes can be tricky, however, especially through walls already closed up. The drawings on these pages present the basics, but there are many different ways to "fish" wires, depending on the circumstances you encounter. For specifics, consult a basic wiring manual. Pay close attention, also, to how wires must connect to boxes; procedures vary according to the type of cable specified by local codes.

First install the boxes and run wires back to the service panel or to the point where you've decided to tap into an existing circuit. Next install the devices, such as receptacles and switches, that go into the boxes. Now turn off the power source and make final connections to it. After you've made all connections, turn power back on and check each receptacle, switch, and fixture outlet with a circuit tester to make sure the device is live and properly grounded. You may choose—or be required by law—to hire an electrician to complete this final stage of an electrical installation.

EXTENDING CIRCUITS

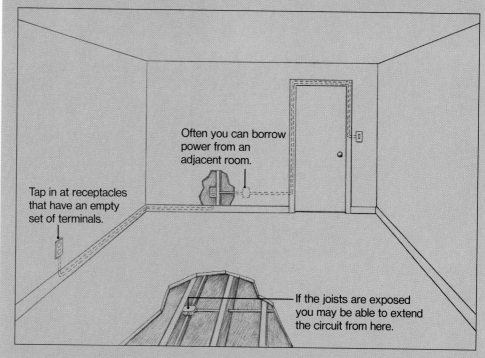

Often you can borrow power from an adjacent room.

Tap in at receptacles that have an empty set of terminals.

If the joists are exposed you may be able to extend the circuit from here.

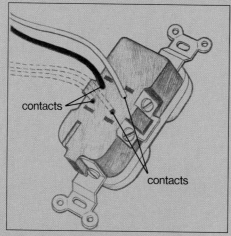

contacts

contacts

Most wall receptacles have two sets of contacts. Attach new cable to an empty set and run it to a new outlet or fixture.

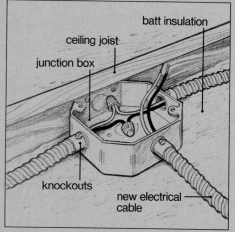

batt insulation

ceiling joist

junction box

knockouts

new electrical cable

A junction box may offer another means to run new cable from an existing circuit, provided it has enough reserve power.

1 Running new cable to a service panel in the basement begins with selecting a spot for a new outlet. Consider its convenience to furniture planned for the room and avoid cutting into a stud. With a keyhole saw, cut the hole to the dimensions of the outlet box.

2 Directly beneath the center point of the outlet hole, drill into the floor at a 45-degree angle to mark the spot where you must drill from below. In a finished room, this means removing the baseboard. Replacing it will cover the hole.

3 Drop a 16d nail through the drilled hole to help you find the spot to drill from below. Down there use a bit with a diameter big enough to pass the cable without squeezing it. Should another partition be directly under the wall, you may have to remove drywall and drill through the top plate and the soleplate, or put the outlet somewhere else.

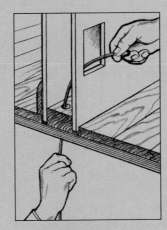

4 Thread wire fish tape up from below, and have a partner catch the hook end and draw it through the outlet hole. This isn't always an easy job, especially if you have to thread fish tape through a combination of walls and floors.

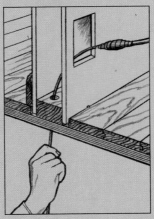

5 Twist together the two lead wires in the cable and slip the fish "hook" over the connected wires. Then, to make sure you don't lose the connection halfway through a wall, wrap the hook and wire with electrical tape. This also ensures a smooth pull.

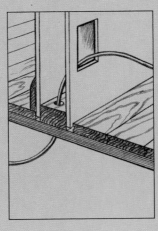

6 Pull the cable into the basement and alongside the service panel, but don't connect it yet. Allow slack for that connection. Go back to the floor above and install the outlet. Make sure all three wires in the cable are properly attached. Put on the plate; connect to the service panel and test your new outlet.

SOLAR
HOT WATER

No longer a dream or an experiment, heating domestic water with solar energy is here. In the United States alone are hundreds of thousands of installations, equipment proven in the field.

Naturally, solar water heaters perform best in areas where clouds only occasionally filter the sun and where cold winters are rare.

Generating hot water accounts for between 11 and 20 percent of the total energy consumed by an average single-family house. A solar hot water heater can save up to 70 percent of that expense.

The drawing *at right* illustrates a typical active system that operates exclusively with water. "Active" means water is pumped into the collector and energy is spent to operate the pump, the compressor, and the sensors. A "passive" system, not shown, operates on a thermosiphoning principle—the natural characteristic of heated water to rise from the collector into a holding tank, and from there by gravity down to the water heater.

Each system also requires a conventional water heater to make up the difference between the solar unit's capability and your household's need.

That a solar hot water heater can cut your fuel bill is a given. Whether the installation cost will be quickly amortized by the savings is another matter. In some situations the payback comes in just a few years. In others, the period could be much longer. Your best course, since so many homeowners now have solar heaters, is to ask someone who's tried one in your area.

Collecting the sun's energy
A typical collector panel—the heart of a system—contains

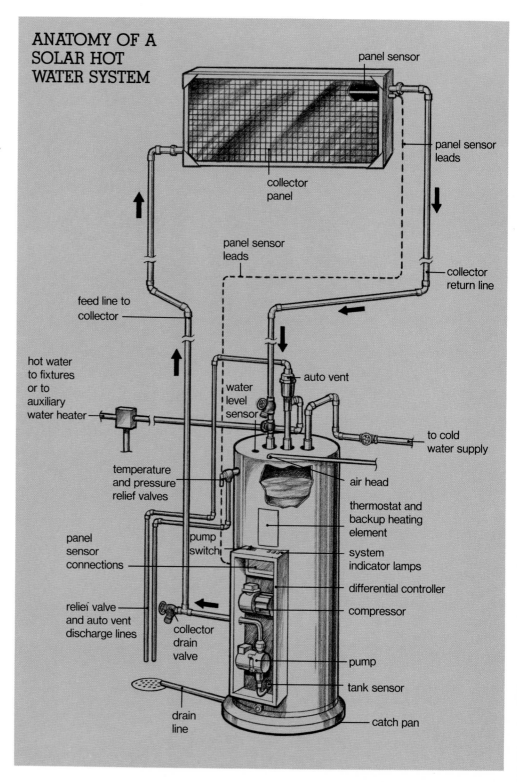

ANATOMY OF A
SOLAR HOT
WATER SYSTEM

panel sensor

collector panel

panel sensor leads

panel sensor leads

collector return line

feed line to collector

hot water to fixtures or to auxiliary water heater

water level sensor

auto vent

to cold water supply

air head

temperature and pressure relief valves

thermostat and backup heating element

panel sensor connections

pump switch

system indicator lamps

differential controller

compressor

relief valve and auto vent discharge lines

collector drain valve

pump

tank sensor

drain line

catch pan

dozens of small-diameter tubes or fluid courses that snake back and forth across the panel surface. When water is the fluid, as it is for the system shown *opposite,* sun-heated water in the panel flows directly to the hot water tank and from there to house faucets.

An alternate system uses an antifreeze solution in the panel piping. Heated, this fluid is directed to coils encircling the hot water tank, from which the tank and subsequently the water draws their heat.

At present, water is more often the fluid used. When danger of freezing is imminent, a sensor opens a valve and the water drains back into the tank, where the supplementary heater takes over.

As the illustrations on this page indicate, the collector panel is always set at an angle, one that approximately equals your community's lati-tude. The object: to direct the panel as closely perpendicular as possible to the sun's position in the sky. The panel must face true south but can be adjusted slightly to the southwest if afternoon sun is warmest.

The drawings here show three ways to mount the panel. In the one *at lower left,* the panel is roof-mounted on its own frame—the method most often used. The frame must be sturdy and open at the bottom so water can run off the roof. The big advantage: a panel can be positioned as specified at the proper angle.

A panel built into the roof system, as shown *at right,* makes sense on a new roof with a slope that's right for the sun's angle.

When codes or sun-blocking obstructions prevent roof mounting, a ground-mounted unit, like the one shown *at lower right,* can be the answer.

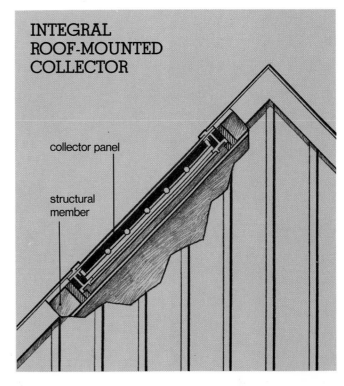

INTEGRAL ROOF-MOUNTED COLLECTOR

collector panel

structural member

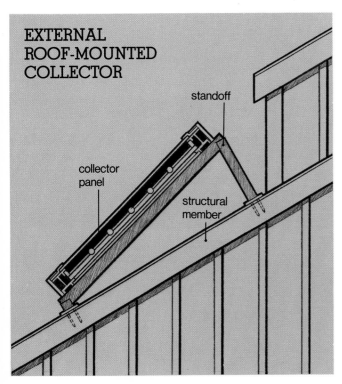

EXTERNAL ROOF-MOUNTED COLLECTOR

standoff

collector panel

structural member

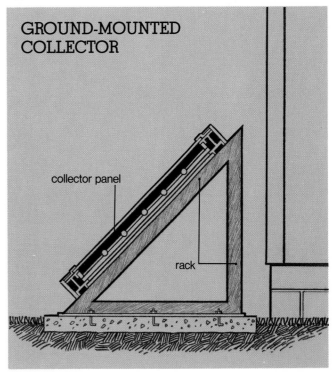

GROUND-MOUNTED COLLECTOR

collector panel

rack

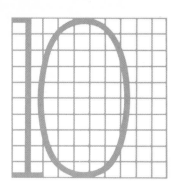

SOLVING GARAGE, BASEMENT, AND ATTIC PROBLEMS

No matter how diverse the architecture and decor of the homes they're part of, basements, garages, and attics are each likely to have certain typical problems. Basements are often dark and damp, garages tend to be boxy and awkwardly placed, and attics—well, if you could just get to them, they'd be great for storage as well as extra living space. Whether your goal is to get the most use out of your garage, basement, or attic in their original versions or to convert the space to another use, you probably need to deal with some of the problems these spaces pose before you can make much progress. This chapter tells how to identify these problems, and gives pointers for solving them.

EVALUATING UNFINISHED SPACES

As you size up the problems and potential of your garage, basement, or attic, keep the following considerations in mind.

• *Light*. Attics and basements are frequently too dark for even minimal use. In attics, this problem can often be overcome by installing a ventilating skylight or windows in end walls, or by building dormers. Even in the basement, you can let the sun shine in with a number of light-admitting construction techniques.

• *Moisture*. Water problems keep many people from using their basements even for storage, but often all it takes to dry out a damp basement is some interior or exterior waterproofing, a dehumidifier, or improved exterior drainage.

• *Ventilation*. If your house isn't equipped with attic or roof-mounted fans, the attic is probably too hot and stuffy for comfort. Add them, along with insulation, to keep air flowing and temperatures down.

• *Access*. In most houses, the garage and basement are easily accessible. The attic may not be so easy to get to. You may want to install disappearing stairs to improve access. To make getting to the basement easier, consider adding an exterior staircase to reach a backyard patio or deck.

• *Structural considerations*. If you're contemplating any kind of conversion, you'll need to pay careful attention to local building, electrical, fire, zoning, and energy codes. For example, to put in an attic floor where one didn't exist before, you may have to beef up the joists underneath; to add dormers and skylights, you may have to move rafters; and if headroom is a problem, you may need to change the placement of cross ties.

MAINTAINING GARAGE DOORS; CLOSING THEM IN

Most of the problems unique to garages have to do with their doors. A door that doesn't go up and down smoothly, that is rotting away at the bottom, or that is leaking energy through poor weather stripping should receive your immediate attention. And if you're planning to convert a garage to living space, one of your first decisions will be what to do with the gaping hole left after the door is removed.

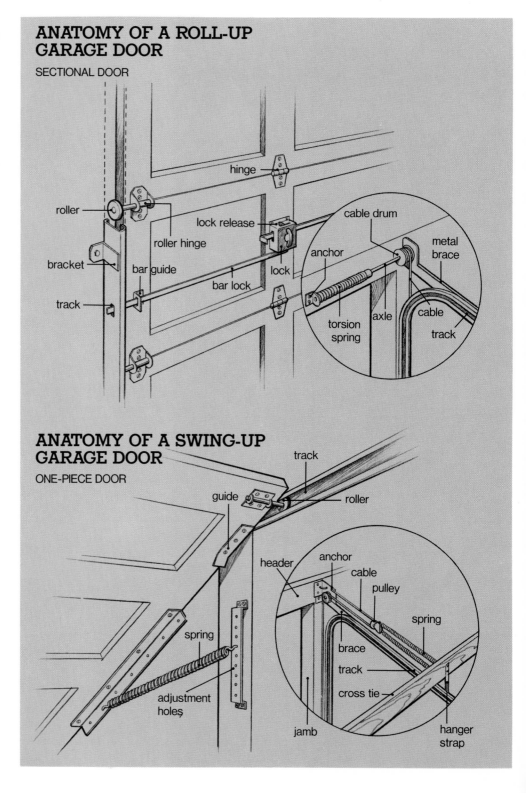

ANATOMY OF A ROLL-UP GARAGE DOOR
SECTIONAL DOOR

hinge

roller

lock release

cable drum

roller hinge

anchor

metal brace

bracket

bar guide

lock

track

bar lock

axle

cable

track

torsion spring

ANATOMY OF A SWING-UP GARAGE DOOR
ONE-PIECE DOOR

track

guide

roller

header

anchor

cable

pulley

spring

brace

spring

track

cross tie

adjustment holes

jamb

hanger strap

Although a garage door is likely to be the largest moving part in your house, the mechanisms that help it move aren't especially complex. As shown in the drawings *opposite,* some swing up all in one piece and others roll up in sections. Both types include tracks and some sort of counterbalancing to assist in lifting them. A third type of garage door, not illustrated, is really two doors that swing on side-mounted hinges; these are like conventional interior doors, only much larger.

When a garage door malfunctions, moisture is usually to blame. It warps doors, rusts hardware, and causes framing members to rot. Keep an eye out for peeling paint on a wood door or rust on a metal one. Blackish marks near the base of a wood door signal rot. If you see any of these signs, improve drainage before serious damage occurs; don't let water build up under or drip onto a door.

Troubleshooting garage doors

Keeping door hardware clean and well lubricated will prevent most problems. Periodically clean grease and oil from tracks and relubricate them with graphite or light oil. Lightly oil hinge pins and rollers, too. Use graphite, not oil or grease, in locksets.

When a door binds, first examine the tracks and the door trim. Built-up grease and dirt in the tracks can cause a door to bind and jump. Also, the tracks must be exactly parallel. Measure between

them in several places and make adjustments if necessary. If the door rubs against its trim molding, either relocate the molding, or adjust or shim out the track brackets.

If the tracks and trim are all right, turn your attention to the counterbalancing system. With pulley-type doors, a slack cable can cause the door to malfunction. If this is the case, tighten the cable, but not so much that it stretches the spring. With swing-up doors, tighten the tension springs by hooking them into the next adjustment hole in the door framing or track support. It's also possible to adjust torsion spring-type doors, but this is not a do-it-yourself job; call in a professional.

When a door won't lock, its bar assembly is probably out of alignment. Adjust either the lockset or the bar guides and keep everything lubricated. If a bar assembly operates stiffly, try rubbing the bars with a crayon or candle.

If a swing-up door sags, its lifting mechanism is probably not strong enough to support the weight. If this is the case at your house, replace—don't try to repair—the mechanisms.

Swinging doors are especially prone to sagging, either because hinges are pulling loose or because a door's own weight is pulling it out of square. Tighten loose hinges by removing them, filling their screw holes with dowels and glue, and replacing the screws with longer screws or

carriage bolts. If a swinging door is out of square, true it up with cable and a heavy-duty turnbuckle. Attach cable to a screw eye at the door's upper corner on the hinge side, install a turnbuckle, and attach the cable's other end to the lower corner on the latch side. Tighten the turnbuckle to square up the door.

Weather-stripping garage doors

Browse through the weather-stripping section of a well-stocked home center and you'll find several products specifically designed to keep water and wind from penetrating a garage door. One, a channel-shape strip of rubber, nails to the bottom of a door, keeping it up off the threshold and compensating for any irregularities that might let in water.

Another garage weather-stripping material consists of a strip of neoprene, T-shape in cross-section, that fits between the panels of a roll-up door. If air is leaking around the sides of a garage door, weather-strip it with a third product; this one is a strip of rubber, bulbous along one edge, that you tack to the door trim.

Tying in a garage conversion

Turning an attached garage into living space can add hundreds of square feet of people-room to your home. Without careful planning and landscaping, however, the exterior of a converted garage can look suspiciously like its former self. The two biggest problems are what to do about the old driveway, and what to do with the tell-tale opening where the garage door is now.

One of the best ways to completely disguise a garage conversion is with landscaping. Planter boxes, shrubs, and even small trees are instant landscaping tools that can help tie everything together. For example, low shrubbery planted along the front and corner of a converted garage will do a lot to soften the lines of the former driveway.

Tearing up a concrete or asphalt driveway and replacing it by seeding or sodding is an expensive proposition. To save money, consider leaving all or part of the driveway in place, adding a privacy fence or plantings, and converting it to a patio or deck.

Dealing with the door

Removing a garage door is a fairly simple procedure, unless the door is equipped with a torsion spring. If yours is, have an expert dismantle the unit. Save the door if you plan to build a new garage.

The large opening created when you remove a garage door will usually let you add enough windows and doors to meet code requirements. When you select new windows and doors, match them in style, materials, and size as closely as possible to the other windows in your house. The same goes for siding. If you can't find the same kind of siding, consider an obviously contrasting material. Before you place your order, however, sketch your ideas to get an idea of the finished effect.

IMPROVING BASEMENT LIGHT AND ACCESS

trim

glass

blocking

Whether your basement does little more than house a washer, dryer, furnace, and out-of-season outdoor equipment, doubles as a hobby center, or is a candidate for conversion to full-time living space, you'd probably like to make several general improvements. Lack of natural light, poor ventilation, and awkward access are classic basement problems. How much they bother you and how you handle them depend on how you use your basement. Even if you have modest plans for your basement, you stand to benefit from making some of the changes suggested here.

The tiny windows at the top of most basement foundation walls are there mainly to meet building code requirements for ventilation and light, but they're rarely enough to truly brighten a basement. Bringing more natural light into an otherwise dark and dreary basement is easier than you might think. In fact, all it takes is a little imagination and some construction ingenuity. You can approach the improvement from several angles.

One technique is to remove some of the blocking between the ends of ceiling joists, as shown *opposite,* and replace it with panes of glass or glass block. The wood blocking adds structural support to the house, of course, so you should check with an architect or experienced contractor before trying this ploy. Keep in mind, too, that replacing blocking with glass will work only if you don't plan to add a ceiling below the basement joists. Painting the joists and ceiling in light colors will amplify the additional light coming in from the outside.

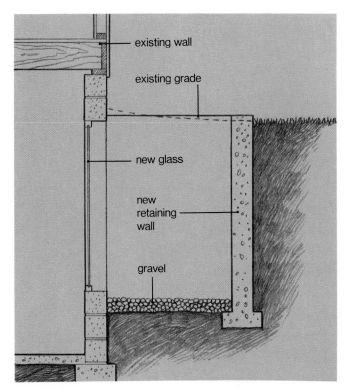

Adding a light well
Another way to bring light—and additional ventilation—into your basement is to excavate and create a light well, like the one illustrated *above.* For lots of light, pick a spot that maximizes exposure to the sun. Outside you'll need a reinforced concrete retaining wall and adequate drainage. Creating a light well, even a small one, involves a good deal of digging, and any modifications to foundation walls call for structural expertise. Contract this job to a professional.

If you'd also like to improve access to your basement, plan a larger light well and add a stairway instead of (or in addition to) a new window. If possible, plan the location of this type of basement entrance so the stairs lead to a patio or deck.

Another way of providing exterior access to your basement is to install a modern-day version of the old cellar door entrance, as illustrated *at left.* Prebuilt metal kit-form doors are easy to install, once you've done the digging, installed stairs, and installed a door in the foundation wall.

Code considerations
If you're thinking about using basement space for bedroom or other living quarters, check first with the local building department. Zoning and building codes vary, but virtually all require ample ventilation and lighting and easy escape in the event of fire. Take special care when you plan the interior and exterior placement of new stairs—most likely the main access sources.

WATERPROOFING A BASEMENT

Water, water every-where! That's the lament many homeowners wail about their basements. Water problems can arise from numerous sources and make basements soggy, smelly, and generally unpleasant. Fortunately, most water-related basement problems are easily dealt with, as you'll discover on these two pages.

At the heart of most basement water problems is a simple physical law: The contrast between temperature below ground (usually a constant 55 degrees Fahrenheit) and the air in the rest of your house and outside creates dampness. Pipes sweat, and when the moisture falls off, puddles form on the floor.

When walls feel damp to the touch, and there's a dank mustiness that never seems to go away, the problems may require a little more work to solve. Moisture created by cracks in foundation walls, faulty mortar joints, ground water forcing its way through the basement walls or floor, and inadequate tiling around and under the foundation are more serious than condensation. If you have a finished basement or are planning to remodel your basement, water problems become especially bothersome. A wall or floor that's even slightly damp can play havoc with paneling and carpeting; constantly damp air can cause mildew.

Finding and solving the problem

All too often a damp basement results from more than one cause—a crack in the wall, inadequate tiling, *and* condensation, for instance. You may even have to go outside the house to check the downspouts from your gutters and the grading along the foundation to find the causes. More about this in the box *below*.

WATERPROOFING A FOUNDATION

1 You'll need a trench that's wide enough to provide adequate working space. Call in a contractor to dig the trench with a backhoe.

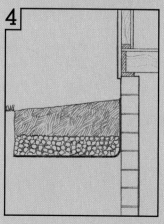

2 When the trench reaches the footings, shore up the trench's sides with heavy lumber to keep earth from caving in or sliding down.

3 Next, coat the wall with asphalt compound and apply heavy-gauge polyethylene. Drape the plastic over the footing and lap all seams at least 6 inches.

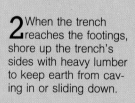
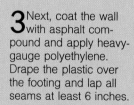
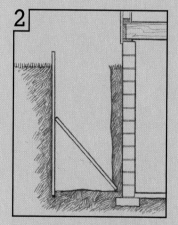
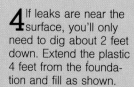

4 If leaks are near the surface, you'll only need to dig about 2 feet down. Extend the plastic 4 feet from the foundation and fill as shown.

There are a number of relatively simple solutions to basement moisture problems. Here's a brief rundown of some of the more common.

• *Pipe insulation.* Wet plumbing lines, typically cold water pipes, can be wrapped with special coverings that insulate the pipe from the air, reduce the amount of condensation, and absorb what does remain.

• *Dehumidifiers.* Just as you might want to add moisture to the air in your house in the winter, you should take moisture out of the air—especially the air in the basement—during the hotter months. Air conditioning reduces humidity, and portable dehumidifiers absorb even more water from the air.

• *Sealing interior walls.* Waterproofing compounds help make a damp, clammy basement wall *seem* dry, but if the moisture problem results from water being forced into the foundation from outside, interior applications will not adhere for long. To be effective, most waterproofing compounds must be applied to clean, *dry* walls, so follow the product manufacturer's instructions to the letter.

• *Plugging holes and cracks.* Cracks in mortar joints and the angle where foundation walls meet the floor can sometimes be patched with quick-hardening expansive cement or epoxy compounds, which can be used even if water is coming in under pressure. Follow the manufacturer's instructions carefully.

If the first fairly simple remedies fail to dry out your basement, you may have to look outside for the solution. Here's when expert assistance will be worth every penny. The box *opposite* shows how to deal with water leaks from the outside.

SOURCES AND SOLUTIONS FOR BASEMENT MOISTURE PROBLEMS

Before you can solve a basement moisture problem, you have to know its cause. Identifying the source of your problems calls for some detective work. Here's how to do some sleuthing, and what to do when you've found the culprit or culprits.

Condensation
Damp walls, dripping pipes, rusty hardware, and mildew may be caused by condensation. To identify condensation, tape a mirror to the dampest part of the wall and wait 24 hours. If after that time the mirror is foggy or beaded with water, suspect condensation.

Condensation is typically caused by excess humidity in the air—usually from an internal source such as a basement shower, washing machine, or unvented dryer—or a significant temperature difference between the wall and the inside air.

To cure condensation, install a dehumidifier, improve ventilation in the basement, or seal the interior walls with a waterproofing compound.

Seepage
Moisture on the floor or a particular wall, especially near floor level, generally is the result of seepage from outside or under the floor. Again, test by taping a mirror to the wall. If moisture condenses *behind* the mirror, seepage is causing the dampness.

With seepage, surface water is forcing its way through pores in the foundation or an expansion joint. The source of this water may be a poorly drained roof or a leaky window well.

Often you can cure seepage by improving surface drainage. If that doesn't work and seepage is relatively minor, an interior sealer may stop the flow. Otherwise, you'll have to waterproof the foundation from the outside, as described in the box *opposite*.

Leaks
Localized wetness that seems to be oozing or trickling from a foundation wall or floor indicates that your basement may be leaking. Check the damp area carefully, paying particular attention to mortar joints between blocks.

Leaks may be caused by cracks that result from normal settling; they may also be caused by poor roof drainage or an outdoor grade that slopes toward instead of away from the exterior basement wall.

You may be able to plug a single hole from inside. If leaks are more generalized, you'll have to dig down and work from outside. To eliminate widespread leaks, waterproof the entire foundation wall and install drain tile around its perimeter.

Subterranean water
Water oozing up from below often shows up as a thin, barely noticeable film on the basement floor. Test for its cause by laying down vinyl sheet goods or plastic for two or three days; if moisture is coming in from below, it will dampen the floor underneath the sheet.

The most common cause of this problem is a spring or high water table that's forcing water up from below under high pressure. This may occur only during rainy periods.

Placing drain tiles around the perimeter of the foundation or floor may help, but only if they direct water to a lower spot or a storm sewer. You may need a sump pump to handle this problem.

HELPING AN ATTIC BREATHE

Every attic, regardless of its role in your home, needs periodic breaths of fresh air. Almost all attics already boast some form of ventilation, included by the builder to minimize condensation that could rot roof framing or wreck insulation. But there's almost always room for improvement, and increasing ventilation up there is one of the easiest and most economical ways to save energy in your home. Improved ventilation not only can reduce your dependence on air conditioning, it also can greatly reduce irksome condensation problems throughout your house.

The drawing *below* illustrates the two main ways to bring outside air into your house: static ventilation systems and power ventilation systems.

Static systems

Static ventilation relies on the fact that hot air rises and draws cooler air behind it—just like a chimney. Your home's doors and windows are good examples of static ventilation. Although these certainly help exchange air, an open door or window wastes a lot of heating or cooling energy by letting hot or cold air escape outdoors.

Many attics already are equipped with *soffit vents* to pull in outside air and have some means for exhausting air, located higher up. Passive exhausting systems might consist of *gable louvers* (or windows), *roof vents,* or a

continuous ridge vent. Passive ventilation is as useful in cool weather as in hot weather, because it keeps air circulating, which in turn prevents moisture from building up. Note that unless a rooftop vent teams up with soffit vents or gable louvers where fresh air can enter, the effect will be minimal.

Power systems

To give nature a boost, power attic ventilators, mounted near the peak of the roof and coupled with air intakes at or near the eaves, pull a strong steady breeze through the attic. This type of ventilating system can reduce cooling costs by as much as 30 percent.
● *Power attic ventilators* are fairly inexpensive and come prewired in lightweight housings that tuck under roofing materials, as shown *opposite.*

Before you purchase a power ventilator, check the manufacturer's specifications to make sure the fan you buy will be big enough to adequately exhaust the air in your attic.
● A *turbine vent* substitutes wind power for electricity. Spun by the wind, a turbine ventilator acts as a fan to draw the air out of the attic.
● A *whole-house fan* installed in the ceiling of a central hallway or at a gable end can cool your home so effectively you won't need air conditioning except on the hottest, most humid days.

HOUSE VENTILATION

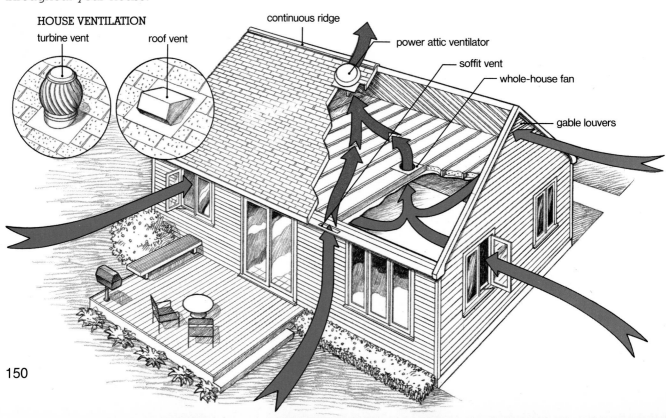

turbine vent

roof vent

continuous ridge

power attic ventilator

soffit vent

whole-house fan

gable louvers

1 Whether you've chosen to install a turbine vent, a roof vent, or a power attic ventilator, install it as close to the peak of the roof as possible. Measure the unit's recommended distance from the ridge down. Find the center of the space between the rafters and drill up through this point.

2 Next, use the hole you drilled through the roof as a guide and scribe a circle the same size as your unit. To cut a circular opening in the top of your roof, use a saber saw with a trammel point attachment. Choose a heavy-duty saw blade designed for cutting rough wood, and cut through the sheathing and shingles.

3 At this point, you should test-fit the ventilator to make sure the opening you've created is large enough. While the unit is resting in the opening, mark around its flashing. Next, remove the ventilator and carefully peel back the shingles around the top and the sides of the hole. As you do this, be sure to leave the building felt in place.

4 To keep the ventilator securely in place and to ensure a tight seal, turn the assembly over and coat its edges with a good grade of roofing cement. Follow the manufacturer's instructions supplied with the unit for securing it to the roof.

5 Cover the back of the unit with roofing cement and slip it into place, with the upper part of the flashing under the rolled-back shingles. On the bottom edge of the ventilator, lap the trailing edge of the flashing over the shingles at the bottom of the opening.

6 After the ventilator is in place, nail its flashing to the roof decking; check the manufacturer's information that comes with the unit for nailing instructions. Apply roofing cement around the flashing and over the nail heads. Finally, restick the shingles you loosened and make power and thermostat connections if necessary.

IMPROVING ATTIC LIGHT AND ACCESS

If you use your attic mostly for storage, you probably aren't too concerned about how much natural light it gets, as long as light bulbs do the job for you. Access is another story, however; if you're carrying large boxes up and down, you want the stairs to be easy to get to and safe to use. And if you use or would like to use your attic as something more than a giant closet, light and access become important. Here are pointers for improving both.

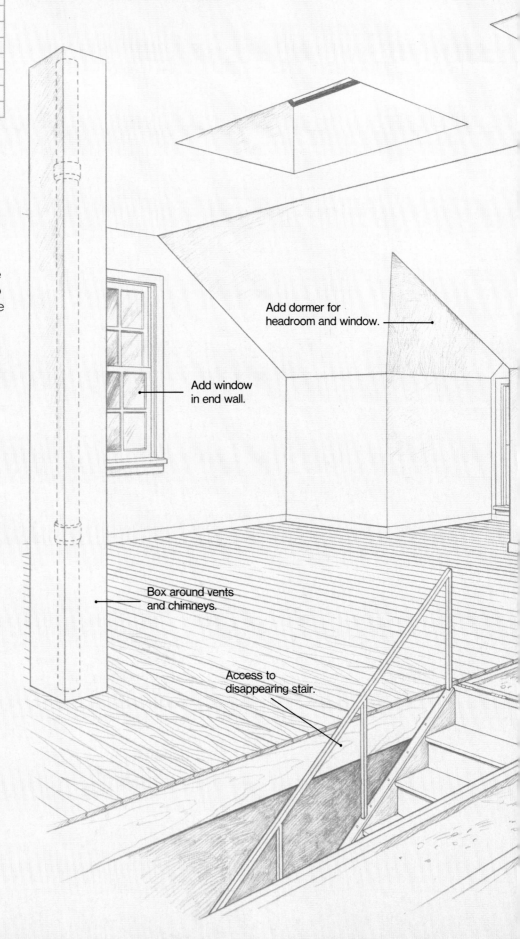

Add dormer for headroom and window.

Add window in end wall.

Box around vents and chimneys.

Access to disappearing stair.

Add venting skylight on roof.

Attics filled with ancestral wardrobes and old photographs are the stuff dreams are made of; so, in many households, are attic conversions—the promise of additional living space at the very top of the house. If, for whatever reason, you're contemplating an attic remodeling, here are some practical aspects to consider.

The best place to start your research is at the local building department. To be certain that your project meets all building, electrical, fire, and energy codes, ask what the requirements are before you start to build. Clearly, more stringent regulations apply to attics used for living space rather than for storage; but some of the areas, notably access, are important no matter what use you want to put your attic to. Here are some of the code specifics you may want to clarify.

• *Window area.* If you want your attic to be legally livable, it probably will have to have a certain number of square feet of window space—exactly how much depends on the square footage of habitable living space in the attic. As a rough guideline, figure that the window area should equal 10 percent of floor space.

• *Ceiling height.* Requirements vary, but generally half of the living area must be at least 7½ feet high. A dormer will increase headroom.

• *Stairs.* Local building codes determine the way stairs are to be built by establishing minimum and maximum dimensions for risers and tread run. Check codes even if you plan to install fold-down or disappearing stairs—these devices are sometimes regulated, too.

• *Skylights.* Although they're a great way to bring light into an attic, adding skylights and windows may conflict with local energy conservation codes. They may also affect the outside appearance of your house. Consider both before deciding to add skylights.

• *Egress.* In case of fire, you'll need a quick and easy escape route from the attic. Check the fire code in your community for requirements about outside exits from attics that are used as sleeping or other living quarters; also determine whether windows can function as exits.

Attic fix-up tips

The drawing *at left* illustrates some ways to make your attic more attractive and usable. Here are some highlights.

• *Pipes.* If you're going to use the attic as finished living space, you'll want to conceal the chimneys and plumbing by boxing them in.

• *Windows.* If possible, add windows to end walls in the attic or dormers for additional ventilation and light. Consider exterior appearance as well as the increased light new windows will contribute to your house.

• *Skylights.* Skylights, created either by building wells in the ceiling to the roof or by using a vented skylight on a sloping roof, provide both light and air.

• *Stairs.* You can improve access to your attic, if it's now unsatisfactory, by building a standard stairway; be sure to consider how the bottom of the stairs might affect traffic patterns on the floor below. If space is at a premium, you can install disappearing stairs, set into a hallway ceiling on the floor below. This is not practical for everyday use, but works well if you use the attic for storing items needed only occasionally.

BEEFING UP AN ATTIC FLOOR

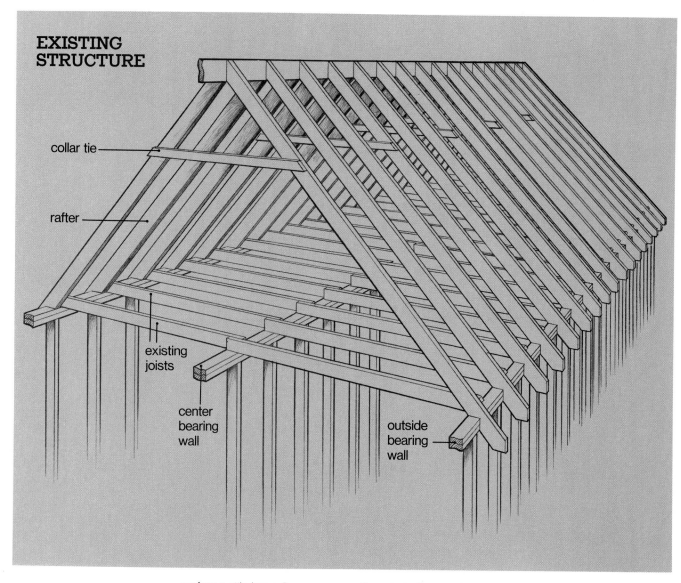

EXISTING STRUCTURE

collar tie

rafter

existing joists

center bearing wall

outside bearing wall

If your attic has a floor, you're already partway through your project. Unless you're planning to store unusually heavy items, you may not have to do much else. And if you plan to use the area as living space, you most likely won't have to do more than cover the current flooring with new carpet, strip flooring, or other floor treatments.

It's not at all unusual, however, to find an attic whose only "floor" is a row of exposed joists. If that's the case at your house, you may have some major construction ahead of you if you want to use the attic for anything at all.

If you're tempted to simply nail plywood or boards to the existing joists and go on from there, resist the temptation. The trouble with this is that the joists themselves, which may

have been sized to do nothing more than bear the weight of the ceiling under them, might be too weak to support a floor above, too. This means that one of the first things you should do is to familiarize yourself with the structural anatomy of your house's upper regions, and the construction terminology shown in the drawing *opposite*. You'll also want to check the local

FORTIFYING JOISTS

AT A CENTER BEARING WALL

Existing joists are typically spliced at center bearing walls. Nail one new joist to an existing one. At the splice and beyond, compensate for the extra space between new and old members with 1½-inch blocking.

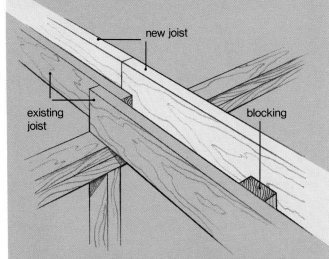

AT AN OUTSIDE BEARING WALL

At an outside wall you'll need to bevel-cut new joists at an angle that conforms with the slope of your home's rafters. Note that you may need blocking between new and old joists here, too.

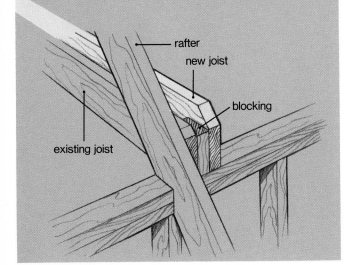

building codes about regulations governing materials used for reinforcing an attic floor, and the recommended joist spacing for various lengths of span.

Once you know the sizes of joists you need, go up into the attic with a flashlight and measuring tape and measure the sizes of existing joists. Bear in mind that a joist's ''nominal'' dimensions measure about ½ inch more than its actual dimensions. A 2x8, for example, actually measures 1½x7½ inches. The discrepancy results from shrinkage when the lumber is dried at the mill.

Numbers to know

The chart *opposite* shows the length of span for different sizes of dimensional lumber installed on 12-, 16-, and 24-inch centers. Use the chart as a guideline, but check local building codes for specific requirements. The thicker the joist, the longer the distance it will span. Thus, using the dimensions in the chart as an example, 2x10 joists set on 24-inch centers can safely span a greater distance than will 2x8 joists set on 12-inch centers.

The size of the joist you choose for beefing up the floor will depend on the amount of weight the floor will carry, plus the weight of the ceiling below. Again, a contractor or the local building department can help you make your selection.

Be aware that simply nailing a joist to another one of the same size won't give you the same strength as you'd get by adding a larger joist. For example, adding a new 2x8 joist to an existing 2x4 joist gives four times the strength that you'd get if you added a second 2x4 to the original.

The drawings in the box *at right* show how new joists are placed alongside the old ones. You'll have to install blocks of wood at the center bearing plate and at the outside bearing wall to compensate for the overlapping of the original joists.

Once you are satisfied that the joists will be strong enough, cover them with ¾-inch plywood or 1-inch lumber subflooring; if the space will be used as a main living area, finished flooring, carpeting, or resilient goods go atop the subfloor.

JOIST SPANS

SPACING	12"	16"	24"
LUMBER SIZE			
2x6	10'	9'	8'
2x8	13'	12'	11'
2x10	16'	15'	14'
2x12	19'	18'	16'

WHERE TO GO FOR MORE INFORMATION

Better Homes and Gardens® Books

Would you like to learn more about changing your garage, basement, and attic into attractive, hardworking living spaces? These Better Homes and Gardens® books can help.

Better Homes and Gardens®
NEW DECORATING BOOK
How to translate ideas into workable solutions for every room in your home. Choosing a style; furniture arrangements; windows, walls, and ceilings; floors; lighting; and accessories. 433 color photos, 76 how-to illustrations, 432 pages.

Better Homes and Gardens®
COMPLETE GUIDE TO HOME REPAIR,
MAINTENANCE, & IMPROVEMENT
Inside your home, outside your home, your home's systems, basics you should know. Anatomy and step-by-step drawings illustrate components, tools, techniques, and finishes. 515 how-to techniques; 75 charts; 2,734 illustrations; 552 pages.

Better Homes and Gardens®
STEP-BY-STEP
BASIC PLUMBING
Getting to know your system, solving plumbing problems, making plumbing improvements, plumbing basics and procedures. 42 projects, 200 illustrations, 96 pages.

Better Homes and Gardens®
STEP-BY-STEP
BASIC WIRING
Getting to know your system, solving electrical problems, making electrical improvements, electrical basics and procedures. 22 projects, 286 illustrations, 96 pages.

Better Homes and Gardens®
STEP-BY-STEP
BASIC CARPENTRY
Setting up shop, choosing tools and building materials, mastering construction techniques, building boxes, hanging shelves, framing walls, installing drywall and paneling. 10 projects, 191 illustrations, 96 pages.

Better Homes and Gardens®
STEP-BY-STEP
MASONRY & CONCRETE
Choosing tools and materials; planning masonry projects; working with concrete; working with brick, block, and stone; special-effect projects. 10 projects, 200 drawings, 96 pages.

Better Homes and Gardens®
STEP-BY-STEP
HOUSEHOLD REPAIRS
Basic tools for repair jobs, repairing walls and ceilings, floors and stairs, windows, doors, electrical and plumbing items. 200 illustrations, 96 pages.

Other Sources of Information

Many professional and special-interest associations publish catalogs, style books, or product brochures that are available upon request.

American Gas Association
1515 Wilson Blvd.
Arlington, VA 22209

American Hardboard Association (AHA)
887-B Wilmette Rd.
Palatine, IL 60607

American Home Lighting Institute
230 N. Michigan Ave.
Chicago, IL 60601

American Plywood Association
P.O. Box 11700
Tacoma, WA 98411

Ceilings and Interior Systems Contractors Association (CISCA)
1800 Pickwick Ave.
Glenview, IL 60025

Exterior Insulation Manufacturers Association (EIMA)
1000 Vermont Ave., NW, Suite 1200
Washington, DC 20005

Gypsum Association
1603 Orrington Ave.
Evanston, IL 60201

National Association of the Remodeling Industry
11 E. 44th St.
New York, NY 10017

Portland Cement Association
5420 Old Orchard Rd.
Skokie, IL 60077

ACKNOWLEDGMENTS

Architects and Designers

The following is a listing by page of the interior designers, architects, and project designers whose work appears in this book.

Cover
R. Schoppet, AIA
Pages 8-9
Atkins Partnership, AIA
Pages 10-11
Kathy Callahan and
Rob Shapiro
Pages 12-13
Paul Pietz, Total
Environmental Action, Inc.
Pages 14-15
Robert A. Harris, AIA
Pages 16-17
Michael Arrington
and David Warrington
Pages 18-19
Davies, Bibbins, Menders,
AIA
Pages 20-21
Paul Bruno Mrozinski, AIA
Pages 22-23
Morsa Studio
Pages 24-25
Doug and Gail Walter
Pages 26-27
Robert Segrest, AIA

Pages 28-29
Constantine Cacos
Pages 30-31
Roberts Architects/Planners
Pages 32-33
Bruce Finkelstein
Pages 34-35
Keith Gross
Pages 36-37
F. Michael Toups, AIA;
R. Franson, Landscape
Architect
Pages 38-39
Ward Bucher
Pages 40-41
Gino Benvenuti,
Benvenuti and Stein
Pages 58-59
Cobbles
Pages 60-61
L. Ward Seymour, AIA,
Dorothy Travis Interiors
Pages 80-83
Georgia-Pacific Corporation
Pages 88-91
Sue Tissue
Pages 92-95
Kent and Robbie Cooper/
Architecture 2
Pages 96-99
Ed Bing
Pages 112-113
R. Schoppet, AIA
Pages 114-115
Case Construction Co.
Pages 122-123
Lynn Nelson and Charles
Peters, The Habitat Center
Pages 126-127
Bob Kirkland, Kirkland/
Ogram and Associates, Inc.

Photographers and Illustrators

We extend our thanks to the following photographers and illustrators, whose creative talents and technical skills contributed much to this book.

Ernest Braun
Ross Chapple
Feliciano
Hedrich-Blessing
Bill Helms
Hopkins Associates
Fred Lyon
Maris/Semel
E. Alan McGee
Ozzie Sweet
Rick Taylor
Jessie Walker

Associations and Companies

Our appreciation goes to the following associations and companies for providing information and materials for this book.

Georgia-Pacific Corporation
The Maytag Company
Viking Sauna

INDEX

Page numbers in *italics* refer to photographs or illustrated text.

A-B

Access, improving, 142
to attic, 19, 72, 153
to basement, *147*
Active solar systems
air, 123
water, *140*
Airtight stoves, *120,* 121
Amperage, calculating, 137
Apartments
attic, *28-29*
basement, *40-41*
Attics, *80, 92-95*
access, improving, 19, 72, 153
anatomy of, *154*
as apartment, *28-29*
code specifics for, 153
floors
beefing up, 82, *155*
building, *82,* 82-83
guest rooms in, *18-21*
guidelines for converting, 72, 153
heating and cooling, 126
insulation, 80-81, *81-83*
as master bedrooms, *10-11, 24-25*
as music room, *22-23*
options for, analyzing, 21, 58
ridge skylight in, *118*
sewing center in, *60*
storage in, organizing, *48-49*
teenagers, remodeling for, *26-27*
planning, *72-75*
ventilation, 142, *150-151*
walls, building, *81*
Basement (drive-under)
garages, family rooms from, *12-13, 30-31*
Basements, *8-9,* 60-61, *61, 76,* 88, *89-91*
apartments in, *40-41*
ceiling treatments, *6-7*
conversion prerequisites, 6
drywall, installing, 78-79, *79*
family rooms in, *38-39, 89*
guidelines for converting, 69
heating and cooling, 126
insulation, *78,* 126

Basements *(contd.)*
light for, 40, 88, 90, *146-147*
moisture problems and solutions, 69, 142, *148,* 148-149
options for, analyzing, 58
storage, inclusion of, in conversion, *54-55*
update of earlier conversion, 90
walls, furring out, 76, *77*
work area, planning for, *68-71*
Baths
in attic suite, *25*
plumbing expansion for, 133
Bearing walls, fortifying joists at, *155*
Bedrooms
attics as, *10-11, 24-25*
closet for, *45*
space for, finding, 11
with wood stove, *115*
Blocking, replacing with glass, *146,* 147
Boot, duct with, *130*
Boxes, electrical, *138*
Breezeways
conversions and additions, *34-35*
as solar system, diagram of, *122*
Btu (British thermal unit) requirements
calculating, 131
insulation and, 126
Building codes, 29

C-E

Cable, running, *138-139*
Carports, building, 98
Car shelter options, 98
See also Garage building
Cathedral ceiling, garage conversions with, 14, *15*
Ceilings
basement, treatment of, *6-7*
garage conversions
cathedral ceiling, 14, *15*
putting drywall on, *85*
Chimney installation for wood-burning unit, *121*

Circuits, electrical
extending, *138*
new, running, *139*
planning diagram, *136,* 137
power for, 137
Clerestory windows, garage with, *112-113*
Closed-loop systems, solar, 123
Closets, improving, *44-46*
Clothes closets, remodeling, *45*
Codes
for attics, 153
building and housing, 29
electrical, 137
Compartmentalized closets, *44*
Computer center in basement, *61*
Condensation in basement, 149
Conduction, 123
Convection, 122-123
Cooling and heating systems, extending, 126, *127-131*
Copper plumbing pipe, 134, 135
Decks, *14,* 114
Dehumidifiers, 149
Den/guest room in attic, *18-19*
Detached garage, connecting, to house, *34-35*
Dining nook in attic, *28*
Divider, room, with storage unit, *54*
Doors
cellar, *147*
garage, 144, 145
anatomy drawings, *144*
in conversion, 52-53, 145
headers for, installing, 104, 105
openers, 110-111
sliding glass, for garage conversions, *12, 30, 31, 98*
Dormers, 25, 93, 95, 116, *117*
building, *116-117*
Drain/waste/vent (DWV)
piping, *133*
installing, *134*
Drive-under garages, family rooms from, *12-13, 30-31*
Driveways
laying out, *102*
treatment of, in garage conversion, 145

Drywall, installing
basement, 78-79, *79*
garage ceiling, *85*
Ducting, *130*
Electrical systems, extending, *136,* 137, *138-139*
for garage conversions, *85*
Entryway for garage conversion, *96,* 97
Extinguishers, fire, 95

F-G

Family rooms
basement, *38-39, 89*
garage, 58, *59*
drive-under garage, *12-13, 30-31*
planning, *64-67*
guidelines for creating, 8
Fireplaces
in basement family room, *38*
in garage family rooms, *13, 59*
installation, *121*
prefabricated, 66, *121*
with storage wall, *52*
types, 121
Fire safety, 95
Fish tape, use of, *139*
Floors
attic
beefing up, 82, *155*
building, *82,* 82-83
basement, options for, 88
brick, *36-37*
garage
building up, 85
installing, *86-87*
oak strip, *32-33*
tile, *30*
Foundations
garage, 102, *103*
waterproofing, *148*
Framing
dormer, *116-117*
garage roof, *106-107*
garage walls, *104-105*
Fresh-air feed fireplace, 121
Furnace options, 128, *129*
wall furnaces, *131*
Furring out walls, 76, *77*

Have BETTER HOMES
AND GARDENS® magazine
delivered to your door.
For information, write to:
MR. ROBERT AUSTIN
P.O. BOX 4536
DES MOINES, IA 50336